SECOND EDITION

Physician Queries

HANDBOOK

Marion Kruse, MBA, RN

Marion Kruse, MBA, RN, Author
Melissa Varnavas, MFA, Editor
Brian Murphy, CPC, Executive Editor
Mike Mirabello, Production Specialist
Matt Sharpe, Senior Manager of Production
Shane Katz, Art Director
Jean St. Pierre, Vice President of Operations and Customer Relations

Advice given is general. Readers should consult professional counsel for specific legal, ethical, or clinical questions.

Arrangements can be made for quantity discounts. For more information, contact:

HCPro, Inc.
75 Sylvan Street, Suite A-101
Danvers, MA 01923
Telephone: 800-650-6787 or 781-639-1872
Fax: 800-639-8511
Email: *customerservice@hcpro.com*

Visit HCPro online at: *www.hcpro.com* and *www.hcmarketplace.com*
Association of Clinical Documentation Improvement Specialists online at: *www.acdis.org*

Contents

CONTENTS

CONTENTS

Online Tools

In addition to the content included in this printed copy, your purchase includes a number of downloadable materials available at the website *www.hcpro.com/downloads/11126*. These materials include:

The 2013 Physician Query Benchmarking Report

The 2010 Physician Query Benchmarking Report

Alternative Sample Physician Query Audit Form

CDI Audit Process White Paper

CDI/Coder Reconciliation Policy

Additional Sample Queries

Introduction: Physician Query Practices Progress

A lot has changed since *The Physician Query Handbook: Guide to Compliant and Effective Communication* was first published back in 2009. Guidance from the American Health Information Management Association (AHIMA) touched on query basics, instructing coders and clinical documentation improvement (CDI) specialists not to "lead" physicians to a particular diagnosis.

At the time of the previous edition's publication, AHIMA's "Code of Ethics" offered one set of rules; its 2001 brief "Developing a Physician Query Process" presented additional direction. In 2008, AHIMA brought forward additional clarification with its "Standards of Ethical Coding" and "Managing an Effective Query Process." With these directives, it aimed to simplify querying practices and to expand its governance to include anyone involved in the process, regardless of professional background.

Since publishing "Managing an Effective Query Process," AHIMA convened a comprehensive committee to draft "Guidance for Clinical Documentation Improvement Programs," in the 2010 *Journal of AHIMA*. It also published a 41-page *Clinical Documentation Improvement Toolkit* and, in the fall of that same year, the *Ethical Standards for Clinical Documentation Improvement Professionals*.

In 2007, the Association of Clinical Documentation Improvement Specialists (ACDIS) was born. Over the next few years, ACDIS created its own "Code of Ethics" modeled after AHIMA and the American Association of Professional Coders and began to publish reports analyzing the latest query practices via benchmarking and surveys of its membership. Since the first publication of this volume, the membership of ACDIS has more than doubled and discussion of query practices has become one of the most important aspects of establishing an effective CDI program. Its members helped draft the 2010 query publications, and in 2012 ACDIS and AHIMA worked collaboratively to create the latest practice brief, "Guidelines for Achieving a Compliant Query Practice." Because it was officially a joint publication, it cemented the applicability of the guidance to CDI and coding/HIM staff members.

But what is a query and why is such a device needed? How has such a simple thing—asking a physician for clarification of the documentation within the medical record—spurred the creation of a whole new profession? According to "Guidelines for Achieving a Compliant Query Practice":

> *A query is a communication tool used to clarify documentation in the health record for accurate code assignment. The desired outcome from a query is an update of a health record to better reflect a practitioner's intent and clinical thought processes, documented in a manner that supports accurate code assignment. The final coded diagnoses and procedures derived from the health record documentation should accurately reflect the patient's episode of care.*

The trouble is, physicians rarely learn about the intricacies of healthcare coding or the documentation requirements coders must adhere to in order to assign a code. They know little, if anything, about how their documentation translates into various code sets for billing, research, and quality control and reporting efforts. When this handbook was first published in 2009, that common language was the International Classification of Diseases, 9th Edition, Clinical Modification (ICD-9-CM). At the time of this publication, CDI and HIM programs have begun preparations for the transition to the 10th Edition, Clinical Modification and Procedure Coding System (ICD-10-CM/PCS) slated for implementation in 2014.

ICD-9-CM contained 24,000 codes. ICD-10-CM/PCS contains more than 150,000. The level of detail required to actually capture the new codes is expected to increase exponentially. Likewise, the importance of CDI and physician query efforts will increase, too.

Nevertheless, the ICD-10-CM draft *Official Guidelines for Coding and Reporting* continues to call for a joint effort between the healthcare provider and the coder to obtain complete and accurate descriptions of the care provided. It states:

> *A joint effort between the health care provider and the coding professional is essential to achieve complete and accurate documentation, code assignment, and reporting of diagnoses and procedures.*

Such hand-in-hand relationships are essential to code assignment and reporting of diagnoses and procedures. In addition, the importance of consistent, complete documentation in the medical record cannot be overemphasized—such sentiments are echoed in nearly every AHIMA query guidance and standards publication, in nearly every government statement regarding query practices, and repeatedly by ACDIS Advisory Board members and throughout its various publications. Without such documentation, accurate coding cannot be achieved. The entire record should be reviewed to determine the specific reason for the encounter and the conditions treated.

INTRODUCTION: PHYSICIAN QUERY PRACTICES PROGRESS

That unique set of skills—the ability to clinically interrogate the medical record while understanding the rules of compliant code assignment—essentially spurred the creation of the CDI profession.

Particular attention must be paid to that concept of "compliance." Since the first publication of this book, a variety of healthcare organizations have come under investigation for inappropriate query practices, including submitting leading queries, upcoding, or other concerns. One facility in Maryland paid more than $3 million to settle fraud allegations. Another group of hospitals paid nearly $9 million.

Furthermore, Recovery Auditors (formerly called Recovery Audit Contractors) target high-volume diagnosis areas and deny claims without supportive clinical evidence in the medical record. Many auditors have even begun to request query forms during their medical record reviews.

The question of what, exactly, constitutes a "leading" query has been subject to much debate throughout the various query guidelines over the years. The most recent ACDIS/AHIMA joint query practice guidance defines a leading query as:

> *One that is not supported by the clinical elements in the health record and/or directs a provider to a specific diagnosis or procedure.*

Throughout *Physician Queries Handbook*, Second Edition, we will address the various government, coding, and industry developments that have shaped CDI and query practices, offer examples of various query forms, and discuss how to craft effective and compliant query policies and procedures. If nothing else, those who purchase this edition should gain an awareness of the importance of creating specific policies and procedures governing facility query efforts. Such policies should be consistent across departments and address processes for query retention, reconciliation, and escalation, among other items.

As indicated in the introduction to the first edition of this book, life is about relationships. For healthcare providers (e.g., physicians, nurses, respiratory therapists, and their extenders) and data quality specialists—as well as HIM and CDI specialists who compliantly interpret, abstract, and code documented clinical information into administrative coded data sets—success is again about relationships.

The relationship of CDI professionals to coders and physicians was a relatively new one back in 2009. At the time, many argued for different query rules depending on the professional submitting the query and the timing—either concurrent or retrospective—of the query. Discussions regarding the best type of query form to use for which diagnosis type also raised questions. Some professionals indicated open-ended, formless queries were best, others opined that only multiple-choice query forms should be used, and still others indicated verbal encounters presented the best option.

Despite the volumes of query advice now available, definitive solutions remain elusive. As the adage goes, the solution is not black or white but rather a shade of gray. Each query submitted must be used to best reflect the conditions and response sought. For example, the latest query guidance permits "yes/no" queries, which will be helpful as CDI specialists and coders work to clarify cause-and-effect relationships needed as ICD-10-CM implementation takes place.

The heart and soul of successful query processes depends on crafting useful policies and effective relationships across departmental lines. It depends on the ability of the provider and the CDI and HIM professionals to be conscientiously and consistently aware of each other's backgrounds, biases, wants, and needs.

Failure to adequately foster this relationship frequently proves detrimental, not only on a personal or even professional level, but also to the very care of the patients themselves. In healthcare, lives really are at stake—even when it comes to appropriate documentation and application of transactional code sets.

There are consequences for failing to understand this critical link between patient treatment and the documentation and coding for such treatment. ICD-9-CM coding based on nonspecific physician documentation has led insurers to raise patient copayments for certain "inefficient" providers, particularly those in tiered networks currently advocated by insurers and increasingly affecting Medicare payments via the hospital value-based purchasing program.

In the same light, coding from nonspecific physician documentation has led to negative publicity for hospitals and their physicians, conveyed via publicly reported mortality data posted on the Centers for Medicare & Medicaid Services' Hospital Compare website or other public websites. Here, some providers have high risk-adjusted death rates for community-acquired pneumonia, heart failure, myocardial infarction, or other conditions based on ICD-9-CM coded data. Communities have witnessed their local hospitals close in part as a result of providers' and coders' inability to negotiate the code-based reimbursement systems that are integral to establishing medical necessity, which is required for accurately assigning diagnosis-related groups for inpatient reimbursement. As the government and the public demand improves quality of care and transparency of data, the physician documentation and coder translation of the medical record becomes almost as vital as the care the patient receives.

Although various stakeholders may not share the same interests or incentives, everyone involved, from physicians to administrators, from program directors to coders and CDI staff, needs a familiarity and empathy for the interplay of each professional's contributions to the cohesion of the healthcare system—to bridge the communication gaps that exist in order to improve the quality of healthcare.

Although reading literature and going to school helps, the best (and sometimes the only) way to learn about another person's world is to ask and listen. Every question deserves a respectful answer.

This book is dedicated to the coders, clinicians, and physicians who diligently work every day to develop and support the professional relationships and processes that are essential to ensure coded data quality.

Special recognition must be made to the authors of the previous edition—Margi Brown, RHIA, CCS, CCS-P, CPC, CCDS; James S. Kennedy, MD, CCS; and Lynne Spryszak, RN, CPC-A, CCDS. Additional appreciation is extended to ACDIS, which sponsored the publication of this edition and donated numerous materials and tools.

As ever, I am grateful to the many colleagues, clients, and peers who continue to challenge me to achieve excellence.

Sincerely,

Marion Kruse, MBA, RN

Healthcare Reimbursement Evolution

In the past 30 years, rules governing healthcare reimbursement in the United States have evolved dramatically as the government attempts to reign in the unsustainable healthcare costs of an aging population. The question of the solvency of the government's healthcare programs has fallen victim to political ideology within the last decade. Total Medicare spending has been projected to increase from $523 billion in 2010 to $932 billion by 2020. From 2010 to 2030, Medicare enrollment is projected to increase from 47 to 79 million, while the ratio of workers to enrollees is expected to decrease from 3.7 to 2.4.[1]

Over the years, the government developed a number of initiatives to handle the dilemma, shifting the focus of payment away from episodic reimbursement to funding based on clinical outcomes and the quality of care provided across the healthcare continuum. In this chapter, we discuss two such payment shifts as representatives of this initiative—the implementation of diagnosis-related groups (DRGs) and pay-for-performance strategies—to highlight the important roles of physician documentation and clinical documentation queries in this landscape.

During the course of changing the way it pays for services, the government has kept its eye trained on inappropriate healthcare billing and outright fraud with the implementation of recovery auditors, Medicare Administrative Contractors, and other efforts (discussed in more depth in Chapter 2).

In this environment, clinical documentation improvement (CDI) program growth has flourished. However, the reasons for such growth are not solely limited to the aforementioned trends. Some are more complex—from implementation of electronic health record systems and computer-assisted coding to the transition to the *International Classification of Diseases, 10th Revision* (ICD-10)—all of which require the capture of specific documentation to be effective.

Add to this the knowledge that data extrapolated from clinical documentation are used in a variety of ways by a variety of organizations—everything from Medicare and Medicaid reimbursement, federal and private quality reporting systems, and even national publications that rank the quality of hospitals and physicians—and the need for accuracy becomes even more important. Yet, the clinical language written by physicians frequently does not match the nuanced language required by coders. Ongoing shifts in healthcare regulatory and reimbursement requirements only increase the challenges coders face in translating physician documentation into applicable codes.

The goal of a compliant CDI program is to address these complex issues by working across departments as translators in order to obtain complete and accurate documentation of the severity of illness and care provided. The primary tool used to accomplish this task is the physician query.

The goal of this book is to review the regulatory infrastructure governing the query process and to outline an approach to help facilities successfully negotiate the communication barriers between providers and facilities in a compliant manner.

Although many tie the exponential growth of CDI programs to the implementation of Medicare severity (MS)-DRGs, retrospective queries have been used for many years by coders and other professionals to facilitate accurate coding. In Chapter 4, we review the evolution of the concurrent query process and CDI. For now, let's look at how the historical changes in healthcare reimbursement led to the vital need for concurrent queries and how current changes in that arena are shifting the focus of CDI efforts.

Advancement of Payment Methods

To understand how clinical documentation influences hospital reimbursement, CDI specialists must first understand how the federal government, through the Centers for Medicare & Medicaid Services (CMS), pays for those services.

In 1965, Medicare reimbursed healthcare based on actual charges. The federal government introduced the inpatient prospective payment system (IPPS) in October 1983 as a way to influence hospital behavior through financial incentives and, in effect, encourage more cost-efficient management of medical care. Three years later, in 1986, CMS created the DRG system. It summarizes the care provided during each patient's stay, grouping up to 24 secondary diagnoses that indicate comorbidities and complications (CC) and up to 25 procedures completed during the patient's stay into a DRG based on the principal diagnosis. The idea was to group diseases together based on comparative costs.[2]

Instead of a payment for each charge submitted, hospitals would receive one predicated sum of money regardless of the number of test performed or length of the hospital stay. By changing the reimbursement system, CMS felt hospitals would be incentivized to control costs and length of stay so they could remain profitable.

GETTING MORE SPECIFIC: A CMS-DRG/MS-DRG EXAMPLE

Under the previous DRG system, congestive heart failure (CHF) unspecified—ICD-9-CM code 428.0—was a CC, and if a physician documented it in the record, and a coder assigned it, there was a change in the DRG.

Under the MS-DRG system, CHF unspecified is not a CC. However, if the physician further clarifies whether the CHF is diastolic (428.30) or systolic (428.20), it becomes a CC. Further, if a physician specifies CHF as acute diastolic (428.31) or acute systolic (428.21) it qualifies as an MCC.

But the catch, as always, is that physicians must be precise with their documentation. For example, documentation of acute left heart failure will not result in a MCC. The words acute diastolic and/or systolic congestive heart failure must be documented to code the MCC. This level of specificity makes an enormous difference in the MS-DRG assigned.

Almost 20 years later, in August 2007, CMS finalized its plans to implement the new MS-DRG system as detailed in the fiscal year (FY) 2008 IPPS Final Rule. More than 700 new MS-DRGs replaced the previous 538 DRGs. It also expanded the CC classification to include major complications and comorbidities (MCC), conditions that require more resources than simple CCs.[3]

In a press release, CMS Acting Deputy Administrator Herb Kuhn stated that Medicare payments for inpatient services "will be more accurate and [will] better reflect the severity of the patient's condition."[4]

CMS said the new system would support facilities caring for sicker patients and would help to prevent abuses:

> Under the old DRG system (with payments based on broad averages) incentives could lead hospitals to cherry pick—the practice of treating only the healthiest and most profitable patients.[5]

One of the more controversial components of the MS-DRG implementation was the assessment of a documentation and coding payment adjustment (DCA), which decreased reimbursement based on the assumption that facilities would see an increase in their case mix index, not due to an actual increase in cases or care provided, but simply due to the more explicit documentation and coding the new system required.

Although some labeled this "DRG creep," many pointed to the improvements as the natural outcome of increased cooperation between the coder and provider to accurately define, document, and code patient conditions using appropriate terminology. In fact, given that hospitals faced a new DRG methodology and across-the-board reimbursement cuts by way of the DCA, many believed that hospitals were being incentivized (and in fact were encouraged by the American Health Information Management Association [AHIMA]) and other professional organizations) to partner with physicians to improve the definition and documentation of treated conditions.

In fact, the 2008 IPPS Final Rule included the following instruction:

> *We do not believe there is anything inappropriate, unethical or otherwise wrong with hospitals taking full advantage of coding opportunities to maximize Medicare payment that is supported by documentation in the medical record.*[6]

Facilities began to find better ways to structure their query processes; to clarify imprecise, illegible, inconsistent, or otherwise incongruent physician documentation; and to refine or implement new concurrent record review and query processes to support the retrospective efforts already in place.

The good news with the new MS-DRG system was that coders would still follow the same principal/secondary diagnosis and procedure coding conventions as before. Furthermore, the MS-DRGs were expected to positively impact profiling and reimbursement for hospitals with a higher case mix index (i.e., more severely ill patients) while requiring more complete and specific information regarding the patient's diagnoses and the care physicians provided. The related Figure 1.1 illustrates the potential opportunity as well as the potential finanical risk.

Although assigning a DRG based on the principal diagnosis and procedure remained essentially the same under the new MS-DRG system, considerable reorientation was needed to understand how the newly added and deleted CCs and MCCs affected secondary-diagnosis assignment and sequencing practices. (Guidance governing such sequencing practices is discussed further in Chapter 3.) And, although the shift to MS-DRGs did not change the coding structure and process, it made various stakeholders along the healthcare chain of command more aware of the diagnostic and documentation specificity required to appropriately capture the right CC/MCC. And, just like the old system, it still takes only one CC or one MCC to change the MS-DRG. In other words, a single element could dramatically alter the clinical picture and the payment related to that case.

4 Physician Queries Handbook, Second Edition

FIGURE 1.1 ◇ EXAMPLE OF A DRG CHART REVIEW

Deficiency	Volume	Revenue Implication
None	34	0
DRG Documentation Opportunity	10	65,867
SOI/ROM* Opportunity	7	n/a
Coding DRG Opportunity	4	$23,452
Coding SOI/ROM* Opportunity	4	n/a
Coding Risk	2	-10,422
Total		$78,897

* Additional documentation or coding would not change the DRG, however, it would change the APR-DRG severity of illness and/or risk of mortality for the case.

Obtaining that level of documentation may require CDI specialists to ask multiple physicians multiple questions to best capture the most appropriate terminology that reflects a patient's severity. Conducting such a volume of questions retrospectively (after the patient has been discharged from the hospital) can prove time consuming, lead to inaccuracies (i.e., the physician does not want to revisit the data and disagrees to make the query go away), and delay final coding and billing. Conversely, performing such inquiries on a concurrent basis, while the patient is still in the hospital under a physician's care, not only hastens the process but also improves the accuracy of the information obtained.

Pay for performance

In 1999, the Institute of Medicine reported that medical errors caused more than 50,000 preventable deaths each year, with an associated cost of $20 billion.[7] The 2006 Institute of Medicine report "Preventing Medication Errors" recommended:

> incentives . . . so that the profitability of hospitals, clinics, pharmacies, insurance companies, and manufacturers (are) aligned with patient safety goals; . . . (to) strengthen the business case for quality and safety.[8]

When healthcare providers receive incentives for performing better—that is, providing better care in a more cost-efficient manner and meeting preestablished targets for the delivery of healthcare—along with disincentives, such as eliminating payments for negative consequences of care (medical errors) or increased costs, the quality of care for Medicare beneficiaries will improve. This is a fundamental change from the traditional fee-for-service and DRG payment methods. The various approaches used to accomplish this agenda are discussed below.

Signed on February 8, 2006, the Deficit Reduction Act (DRA) required CMS to identify hospital-acquired conditions (HAC) that:

- Are high cost, high volume, or both

- Result in the assignment of a case to a DRG that has a higher payment when present as a secondary diagnosis

- Could reasonably have been prevented through the application of evidence-based guidelines are a CC or MCC for the MS-DRG system[9]

In addition, as of October 2007, CMS began requiring assignment of present-on-admission (POA) indicators. The goal of the POA indicator is to better define clinical conditions or consequences that arise during an inpatient admission. Reporting options include:

- Y = present at the time of inpatient admission

- N = not present at the time of inpatient admission

- U = documentation is insufficient to determine whether condition is POA

- W = provider is unable to clinically determine whether condition was POA

- Unreported/not used (or "1" for electronic billing) = exempt from POA reporting

Figure 1.2 illustrates one possible query template that CDI professionals may use to clarify whether a particular diagnosis was POA.

It allows CMS to identify whether an HAC is POA. If it was not (or documentation is insufficient to determine) the diagnosis does not qualify as a CC or MCC for the MS-DRG assigned. Moreover, if it is the only CC or MCC, the case is assigned to the lower paying MS-DRG, and hence penalizes hospitals with poor quality.

FIGURE 1.2 ◇ SAMPLE POA QUERY FORM

Clarification is needed for one (or more) of the following conditions in order to accurately assign the "present on admission" indicator. Please check the box that indicates whether the associated condition was present at the time of the order for inpatient admission.

Y	N	U		W
Yes	No	Unknown		Clinically Unable to Determine
❏	❏	❏	❏	_____
❏	❏	❏	❏	_____
❏	❏	❏	❏	_____
❏	❏	❏	❏	_____
❏	❏	❏	❏	_____
❏	❏	❏	❏	_____
❏	❏	❏	❏	_____
❏	❏	❏	❏	_____

Please sign and date below:

_____   _____

Physician signature   Date

Source: Physicians Queries Handbook, First Edition.

In 2010, the Affordable Care Act required the U.S. Department of Health and Human Services to establish a value-based purchasing (VPB) program for inpatient hospitals and, on May 6, 2011, CMS published the VBP Final Rule. Whereas the CMS Hospital Inpatient Quality Reporting (IQR) program is a pay-to-report structure (i.e., hospitals receive payments for reporting data), the VBP program provides financial incentives based on adherence to process and outcomes. It acts in tandem to the IQR.

Starting in FY 2013, CMS began withholding 1% of the base operating MS-DRG payment for each discharge, with plans to gradually increase the amount withheld to 2% by FY 2017. This allows CMS to create a pool of money that is then used to reward hospitals with higher quality.[10]

The initial 2013 VBP program adopts performance measures under the following two "domains":

1.   Clinical process, composed of 12 measures

2.   Patient experience, composed of the Hospital Consumer Assessment of Healthcare Providers and Systems survey[11]

Hospitals are evaluated based on whether they met the performance standards for the measures by comparing their performance during the performance period to their performance during a three-quarter baseline period. Each hospital is scored based on achievement and improvement ranges for each measure. Then a total performance score is calculated by combining the greater of the hospital's achievement or improvement points for each measure to determine a score for each domain.

CMS then converts each hospital's total performance score into a value-based incentive payment utilizing a linear exchange function.

Furthermore, Section 302 of the ACA established the Hospital Readmissions Reduction Program. Beginning in 2013, hospitals with excess 30-day readmissions for patients with acute myocardial infarction

---

PERFORMANCE SCORING PLANS

For the final score, each domain score is weighted as follows:
2013:
  1.   Clinical process of care: 70%
  2.   Patient experience of care: 30%

2014:
  1.   Outcome domain = 30%
  2.   Clinical process of care domain = 20%
  3.   Patient experience of care domain = 30%
  4.   Efficiency domain = 20%

(AMI), heart failure (HF), and pneumonia (PNA) will see a reduction in overall base DRG payments. This program requires CMS to monitor readmissions to the same or another acute care hospital that occur within 30 days and are in the DRGs monitored. Readmissions within these targets are risk adjusted and calculated as a ratio of actual versus expected readmission. Again, although the program only includes the DRGs for AMI, HF, and PNA, a hospital's base rate for _all_ DRGs during the fiscal year will be decreased (penalized) or increased (rewarded).

Beginning in 2014, CMS will add two more domains the hospital VBP scoring methodology. First, an outcome domain will be added that encompasses 30 day mortality rates for AMI, HF, and PNA. Second, an efficiency domain will be added that measures Medicare spending per beneficiary (MSPB). This second measure includes all Medicare Part A and B payments from three days prior to admission through 30 days post discharge. Both domains are risk adjusted to account for the severity of illness of the patient.

Lastly, in 2015, a portion of Medicare payments will be linked to effective implementation of electronic health records (meaningful use) and the HAC program will be moved from the IQR to the VBP program. As part of this move, hospitals will be assigned an aggregate HAC score which will be combined with the hospital's score on other outcome measures to derive an outcome domain score. Although most of the outcome domain measures are risk adjusted, HAC measures are not. Figure 1.3 illustrates how these payment reductions will play out over time.

Under such financial constraints, facilities need to have a mechanism to concurrently assure accurate physician documentation and information collection and promote collaborative efforts among medical staff, coders, CDI, case management, and quality team members.

Still not convinced?

Additional pay-for-performance initiatives made headlines in early 2013 when New York City's Health and Hospitals Corporation, the nation's largest public health system, entered into negotiations with its physician unions to tie bonuses of nearly $60 million through 2016 to their quality measures.[12]

Although the onset of MS-DRGs may have increased the need for CDI efforts, the implementation of VBP is changing the focus of those programs dramatically away from CC/MCC capture rates ("one and done") and case-mix index ratios to one focused on capturing the complete specificity of the entire medical record and facilitating documentation improvement conversations across departmental lines.

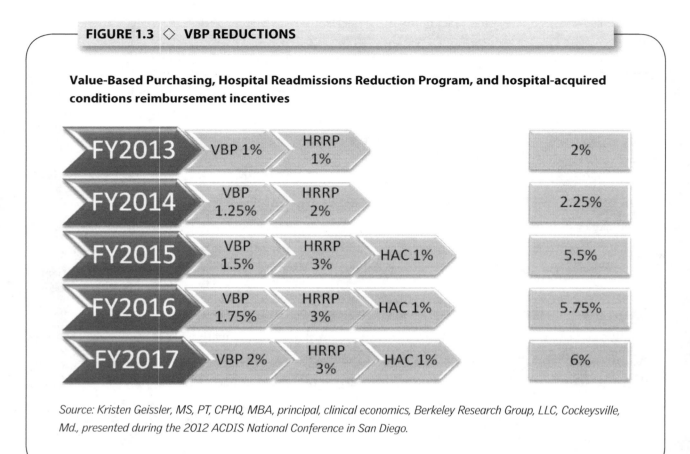

FIGURE 1.3 ◇ **VBP REDUCTIONS**

Value-Based Purchasing, Hospital Readmissions Reduction Program, and hospital-acquired conditions reimbursement incentives

Source: Kristen Geissler, MS, PT, CPHQ, MBA, principal, clinical economics, Berkeley Research Group, LLC, Cockeysville, Md., presented during the 2012 ACDIS National Conference in San Diego.

To make such a shift requires programmatic changes for CDI professionals. It may require additional staffing or changes to productivity requirements. It may require additional education for CDI specialists and physicians or changes to institutional query forms to incorporate elements of the VBP initiative.[13]

Regardless, facilities with CDI programs and query efforts in place will undoubtedly fare better than those without any concurrent review and query program. Those programs that continue to focus solely on CC/MCC capture will need to expand and recalibrate their query efforts to include documentation that supports POA, quality, and risk adjustment.

All these changes speak to the importance of CDI programs, including a need for a structured concurrent and retrospective physician query processes. In fact, one of the greatest challenges essentially comes from helping physicians understand the reporting language of the clinical care they provide. The rest of this book explores how to accomplish concurrent and retrospective queries in a compliant manner that promotes accurate DRG, quality, and VBP reimbursement.[14]

REFERENCES

1. Centers for Medicare & Medicaid Services (CMS). *The 2011 Annual Report of the Boards of Trustees of the Federal Hospital Insurance and Federal Supplementary Medical Insurance Trust Funds. www.cms.gov/Research-Statistics-Data-and-Systems/Statistics-Trends-and-Reports/ReportsTrustFunds/downloads/tr2011.pdf.* Accessed February 2013.

2. CMS. Acute Care Hospital Inpatient Prospective Payment Fact Sheet, p. 2. *www.cms.gov/MLNProducts/downloads /AcutePaymtSysfctsht.pdf.* Accessed November 2011.

3. Ibid.

4. CMS. Press Release. "CMS announces payment reforms for inpatient hospital services in 2008." August 1, 2007. *www.healthcare .philips.com/pwc_hc/us_en/about/Reimbursement/assets/docs/Overallcmspressreleaseonfinal08inprule.pdf.* Accessed February 2013.

5. Ibid.

6. CMS. 2008 *Inpatient Payment Prospective System Final Rule,* p. 208. *www.cms.hhs.gov/AcuteInpatientPPS/downloads/CMS-1533-FC .pdf.* Accessed February 2013.

7. Institute of Medicine. "To Err Is Human." The National Academies Press. November 1999. *www.iom.edu/Reports/1999/To-Err-is-Human-Building-A-Safer-Health-System.aspx.* Accessed February 2013.

8. The Institute of Medicine. "Preventing Medication Errors." The National Academies Press. July 2006. *www.iom.edu/Reports/2006 /Preventing-Medication-Errors-Quality-Chasm-Series.aspx.*

9. CMS. Hospital Acquired Conditions Fact Sheet. *www.cms.gov/Medicare/Medicare-Fee-for-Service-Payment/HospitalAcqCond/index .html?redirect=/hospitalacqcond.*

10. CMS. "FAQ: Hospital Value Based Purchasing," p. 8. *www.cms.gov/Medicare/Quality-Initiatives-Patient-Assessment-Instruments /hospital-value-based-purchasing/Downloads/FY-2013-Program-Frequently-Asked-Questions-about-Hospital-VBP-3-9-12.pdf.*

11. Association of Clinical Documentation Improvement Specialists (ACDIS). "Value-based purchasing presents new CDI opportunities." *CDI Journal,* July 2011, Vol. 5, No. 3, p. 13. *www.hcpro.com/content/268140.pdf.*

12. Hartocollis, A. "New York City Ties Doctors' Income to Quality of Care," *The New York Times,* January 11, 2013. *www .nytimes.com/2013/01/12/nyregion/new-york-city-hospitals-to-tie-doctors-performance-pay-to-quality-measures.html?pagewanted= 1&nl=todaysheadlines&emc=edit_th_20130112&_r=1&.*

13. ACDIS. "Value-based purchasing presents new CDI opportunities." *CDI Journal,* July 2011, Vol. 5, No. 3, p. 13. *www.hcpro.com/content/268140.pdf.*

14. Ibid.

Regulatory Environment

The advancement of clinical documentation improvement (CDI) efforts brings with it unique challenges. As benevolent a mission as CDI may seem to have, for many facilities the focus of concurrent physician queries continues to be "optimizing" information in the medical record in order to increase reimbursement. When such efforts do not reflect the care provided to the patient, these practices could be construed as fraud—particularly when data patterns appear to illustrate inconsistencies with national norms.

When AdvanceMed Corporation, the Zone Program Integrity Contractor (ZPIC) for the Centers for Medicare & Medicaid Services (CMS), parsed its data, it identified eight aberrant providers all essentially from the same healthcare system. After years of investigations and subsequent negotiations between the facilities and the U.S. Department of Justice (DOJ), the facilities ultimately paid an $8.9 million settlement. The DOJ found, in most cases, "the timing of changes in peer comparison data—from below average/average to above average—coincided with implementation of CDI programs".[1]

Similarly, when a 2005 Maryland qui tam case settled for nearly $3 million in June 2009, prosecutors pointed to CDI efforts related to leading queries at the crux of the allegations.[2]

Of course, healthcare providers must ensure the financial solvency of their organizations, just as government officials must ensure the solvency of their healthcare funding programs. Both sides of this fiscal conundrum face growing financial frustration, as both sides continue to search for an underlying cause to answer the dilemma of expanding healthcare costs. Nevertheless, when a facility submits a claim to the federal government for payment of activities that were never provided, it risks being accused of False Claims Act (FCA) violations, investigations by the Office of Inspector General (OIG), and, in some cases, such as those described above, prosecution by the DOJ.

False Claims Act

The foundation for healthcare compliance comes from the FCA, which was originally enacted during the Civil War to combat the fraud perpetrated by companies that sold supplies to the Union Army. At the time, war profiteers shipped boxes of sawdust instead of guns and swindled the Union Army into purchasing the same horses several times.

Although investigators use the FCA to prosecute crimes from any number of possible avenues, healthcare fraud and abuse remains among the top uses of the law today. The FCA:

> *Imposes liability on those who make false statements or claims for reimbursement to the government.*

Under the FCA, individuals can be held liable if they are found guilty of:

- "Knowingly presenting or causing to be presented . . . a false or fraudulent claim for payment or approval

- Knowingly making a false record or statement (or causing a false record or statement to be made) in order to get a false or fraudulent claim paid or approved by the government

- Conspiring to defraud the government by getting a false or fraudulent claim allowed or paid"[3]

If found guilty, it could mean a civil penalty of not less than $5,000 and not more than $10,000, plus *three times* the amount of damages the government sustains because of the act of the guilty party.

In the law, the terms "knowing" and "knowingly" mean that an individual:

- Has actual knowledge of the information

- Acts in deliberate *ignorance of the truth* or falsity of the information

- Acts in reckless disregard of the truth or falsity of the information

No proof of specific intent to defraud is required.

As an incentive to bring such fraudulent activities to the government's attention, the FCA contains the "qui tam" provision, which permits citizens to sue on behalf of the government and be paid a percentage of the recovery. If the suit is successful, the "relator" may receive at least 15% but not more than 25% of the proceeds of the action or settlement of the claim, depending on the extent to which the person substantially contributed to the prosecution of the action.[4]

Such was the suit brought against Johns Hopkins Bayview Hospital in Maryland. Relators in the case alleged Bayview added secondary diagnoses that did not exist in order to increase reimbursement. Furthermore, the relators claimed that cases were screened by a physician member of the CDI team who submitted leading queries based on transitory test results in certain areas like malnutrition and acute respiratory failure that could be construed to indicate the presence of certain secondary conditions that were not actually diagnosed or treated during the patient's hospital stay. And, according to the suit, the physician advisor later worked directly with the billing department, amending documentation that did not comply with previous query requests and pressuring coders to add secondary diagnoses even if they disagreed based upon their review of the medical record as a whole.[5]

The question of what, exactly, constitutes a "leading" query has been of one of much debate over the years. The most recent joint query practice guidance from the Association of Clinical Documentation Improvement Specialists (ACDIS) and the American Health Information Management Association (AHIMA) defines a leading query as:

> *One that is not supported by the clinical elements in the health record and/or directs a provider to a specific diagnosis or procedure.*[6]

Nevertheless, the OIG and CMS historically viewed physician queries with some skepticism. They depicted queries as efforts to "lead" the physician or introduce "new information" to the medical record in an effort to increase reimbursement. A good example of this skepticism derives from the OIG's investigations of pneumonia coding in the late 1990s. In many cases, the OIG depicted the physician query process as an effort to "upcode" a patient's diagnosis improperly.

Upcoding means billing for a code with a higher reimbursement rate than the code that actually reflects the service furnished to the patient. Another frequently used term, assumption coding, means assuming (and coding) certain conditions or treatments in the absence of the physician's explicit documentation of that diagnosis or treatment.

The OIG recounted its findings from the pneumonia upcoding investigation in a 2006 report, "Protecting Public Health and Human Services Programs: A 30-Year Retrospective." In its review of more than 100 hospitals, the agency found that most cases should have been assigned a lower-paying DRG based on physician documentation. Following the investigation, 34 hospitals entered into corporate integrity agreements and paid more than $35 million to settle respective FCA liability.[7]

Additional fines related to FCA violations

Supporting the FCA is the Civil Monetary Penalties Act, which assesses damages, in addition to any other penalties that may be prescribed by law, to a civil monetary penalty of not more than the following:

- $10,000 for each item or service

- $15,000 for each individual with respect to whom false or misleading information was given

- $10,000 for each day the prohibited relationship occurs

- $50,000 in other circumstances

In May 1995, a two-year demonstration project dubbed Operation Restore Trust (ORT) joined the OIG, CMS, DOJ, and Medicare and Medicaid contractors to address healthcare billing fraud and abuse using the FCA and the Civil Monetary Penalties Act. In two years, the demonstration project:

- Identified $23 in recoveries for every $1 spent on ORT

- Identified more than $187.5 million in fines, recoveries, settlements, and civil monetary penalties owed to the federal government

- Achieved 74 criminal convictions, 58 civil actions, and 69 indictments

- Excluded 218 providers from participation in federal healthcare programs[8]

Public Law 95-452 authorizes the OIG to protect the integrity of CMS programs, as well as the health and welfare of the beneficiaries of those programs. The OIG routinely audits facilities and providers according to priorities outlined in its annual *Work Plan*.[9] Where other agencies recover only overpayments, the OIG has the authority to rescind an entity's or individual's privilege to receive reimbursement for services rendered to those participating in Medicare or Medicaid.[10]

Enforcement Efforts Evolve

Many CDI professionals believe that education alone promotes physician and facility compliance with federal rules and regulations regarding clinical documentation. Consider, however, how many individuals exceed the speed limit in their automobiles as they drive down the freeway, even though there are educational signs every mile or two prompting them to comply with the law. If it were not for law enforcement personnel and their authority to mete out consequences, many would consider speed limits as suggestions rather than rules. The same is true with healthcare compliance. The results of the ORT illustrate that fact. With such returns validating the importance of enforcement, a host of additional regulatory agencies with assorted acronyms followed over the years, including:

- PEPP (Payment Error Prevention Program)

- HPMP (Hospital Payment Monitoring Program)

- PEPPER (Program for Evaluating Payment Patterns Electronic Report)

- RAC (Recovery Audit Contractor)

- MAC (Medicare Administrative Contractor)

PEPPER use

Some of these programs actually provide concrete data to help facilities identify potential improvements, such as PEPPER, for example, which defines risks for payment errors (referred to in the report as "target areas") against national reporting norms. In addition, the quarterly report then compares individual facility data to state and fiscal intermediary/MAC regional information and highlights which diagnoses represent outliers for an organization.

PEPPER is distributed via MyQualityNet to hospital administrators. CDI staff can work with their hospital's QualityNet administrator to obtain a basic user account. They should ask for "PEPPER recipient" and "file exchange and search" roles.

It flags when a hospital is at or above the 80th percentile in billing for a particular risk area—meaning, when the hospital submits a higher percentage of claims for that risk area than 80% or more of the hospitals in that comparison area (i.e., state, MAC, or national). Such comparisons enable a hospital to determine whether it is an outlier—that is, whether it differs significantly from other similar facilities. When a facility has a "red flag," it can be used to guide the development of their internal audits and to improve all aspects of documentation, coding, and ultimately patient care.

The reports also include:

- Interpretive guidance on each target area

- Suggested interventions

- Improved labeling of time periods on the target area worksheets and graphs

Many of the PEPPER targets mirror those of CDI programs and include items such as:

- Septicemia

- Respiratory infections

- Stroke/intracranial hemorrhage (ICH)

- Simple pneumonia

Additional target areas include:

- Unrelated operating room procedures

- Surgical DRGs with CC/MCC

- Excisional debridement

- Ventilator support

- Transient ischemic attack (TIA)

- Chronic obstructive pulmonary disease (COPD)

- Percutaneous transluminal coronary angioplasty (PTCA) with stent

- Syncope

- Other circulatory system diagnoses

- Other digestive system diagnoses

- Readmissions

- One-day stays

- Two-day stays

Armed with this data, CDI specialists can consider additional query educational opportunities to reduce discrepancies if warranted.[11]

Recovery Auditors

Formerly known as RAC, the Tax Relief and Health Care Act of 2006 created Recovery Auditors to identify Medicare overpayments and underpayments made on claims of healthcare services provided to Medicare beneficiaries. Overpayments occur when healthcare providers submit claims that do not meet Medicare's coding or medical necessity policies. Underpayments occur when healthcare providers submit claims for a simple procedure but the medical record reveals that a more complicated procedure was actually performed. However, contractors receive compensation for their efforts based on a percent of the claims they recover and are therefore incentivized to target overpayments, critics say. In fact, in 2012, the American Hospital Association filed a lawsuit against CMS claiming that its denial practices violate federal law.[12]

As illustrated in Figure 2.1, however, the latest CMS report to Congress (submitted in February 2013 for fiscal year [FY] 2011), Recovery Auditors saved Medicare nearly $500 million, an increase from $92.3 million in combined overpayments and underpayments identified and corrected in FY 2010 [13].

Recovery Auditors need CMS's approval to pursue record reviews for specific DRGs, and each contractor must publish its focus areas publicly. So, CDI programs have similarly identified these areas of concern and added these reviews to their "to-do" lists. For example, CDI program directors should pull

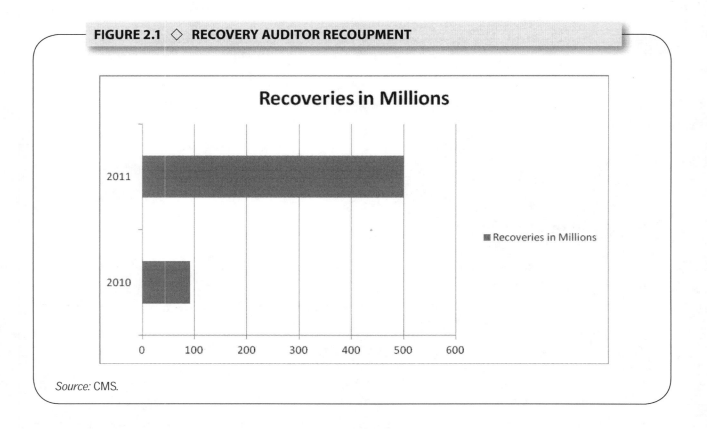

FIGURE 2.1 ◇ RECOVERY AUDITOR RECOUPMENT

Recoveries in Millions

Source: CMS.

MS-DRG lists by frequency and compare their top DRGs to the list of target areas identified by their regional auditor.[14]

Despite Recovery Auditors' reported success in recouping and clarifying Medicare claims, the American Hospital Association (AHA) finds that when hospitals appeal their denials, they typically win. AHA's *RAC Trac Report* indicates that hospitals appeal more than 40% of their denials with a roughly 75% success rate.[15]

Although MAC have been conducting prepayment reviews for some time, Recovery Auditors reviewed claims only on a retrospective basis—that is until CMS announced a prepayment review demonstration project that launched at the end of August 2012.[16]

Such recoupment efforts provide yet another reason for the implementation and expansion of CDI query efforts, with 32% of CDI programs conducting reviews to audit-proof their records from Recovery Auditor targets, according to a 2012 poll.[17]

To handle those audits and prepare their facilities, CDI specialists increasingly have migrated into an audit prevention and analysis role. Prepayment targets during the demonstration portion targeted the following MS-DRGs:

- 312, Syncope and collapse

- 069, Transient ischemia

- 377, GI hemorrhage with MCC

- 378, GI hemorrhage with CC

- 379, GI hemorrhage without CC/MCC

- 637, Diabetes with MCC

- 638, Diabetes with CC

- 639, Diabetes without CC/MCC

Furthermore, although Medicare Quality Improvement Organizations (QIO) maintain statutory authority to monitor the medical necessity of inpatient admissions,[18] Recovery Auditors expanded their reviews to medical necessity in FY 2011.[19]

Nevertheless, QIOs provide yet another layer of government oversight.

By law, the QIO's mission is to improve the effectiveness, efficiency, economy, and quality of services delivered to Medicare beneficiaries. Its core functions, according to CMS, include:

- Improving quality of care for beneficiaries

- Protecting the integrity of the Medicare Trust Fund by ensuring that Medicare pays only for services and goods that are reasonable and necessary and that are provided in the most appropriate setting

- Protecting beneficiaries by expeditiously addressing individual complaints[20]

To complicate matters further, Recovery Auditors began requesting queries along with their medical record reviews. Those CDI programs that had no policies in place struggled to determine whether their facility considered queries a permanent part of the medical record, and therefore recoverable by auditors, or whether queries were business records related to the care and therefore possibly not required for submission. Additional concerns regarding query permanence are addressed later in this book.

Compliance Involvement in CDI Efforts

CDI programs bear the weight of potentially great benefit or potentially great risk for their organizations, depending on the focus and compliance of their query efforts. Subsequent chapters address the rules governing CDI query practices and the role of policies and procedures in ensuring compliance. It is worth mentioning here, however, that CDI programs should include input from their facility compliance officer and legal council at various stages of implementation and growth.

Ongoing compliance department involvement can help ensure that CDI queries are structured in a compliant manner and can advise the CDI staff members as to whether templated queries are acceptable. Such involvement will help guarantee that your CDI program meets the doctrine and spirit of the existing regulations.

Because CMS represents the nation's largest healthcare payer, many CDI programs get their start in conducting record reviews for Medicare patients and/or top diagnosis target areas. However, the goal of improved documentation and patient care should be consistent across payers and disease type, not just improved healthcare documentation for patients who happen to have government insurance. In addition, the goal of improved documentation and patient care should not focus only on high-cost services such as acute respiratory failure or any other special circumstance. When there is a lack of consistency in policies and procedures, for example, reviewing Medicare and not private payers, the risk for potential misuse and abuse increases.

REFERENCES

1. Morris S.B., Benjamin S., Schecter J.D. "Medicare Claims Recoupment: Case Study of Department of Justice Settlement." Association of Clinical Documentation Improvement Specialists 5th Annual Conference, May 2012. *www.hcpro.com/content/280217.ppt.*

2. Bennett, J. "Legal aspects of CDI: A case study." Association of Clinical Documentation Improvement Specialists 4th Annual Conference, May 2011. *www.hcpro.com/content/264933.ppt.*

3. Department of Justice. "The False Claims Act: A Primer." *www.justice.gov/civil/docs_forms/C-FRAUDS_FCA_Primer.pdf.*

4. Ibid.

5. Bennett, J. "Legal aspects of CDI: A case study." Association of Clinical Documentation Improvement Specialists 4th Annual Conference, May 2011. *www.hcpro.com/content/264933.ppt.*

6. American Health Information Management Association (AHIMA). "Guidelines for Achieving a Compliant Query Practice." *Journal of AHIMA*, Vol. 84, No. 2, February 2013. *http://library.ahima.org/xpedio/groups/public/documents/ahima/bok1_050018. hcsp?dDocName=bok1_050018.*

7. Office of Inspector General (OIG). "Protecting Public Health and Human Services Programs: A 30-Year Retrospective." *https://oig .hhs.gov/reports-and-publications/retrospective.asp.*

8. Department of Health and Human Services. Press release. "Secretary Shalala Launches New 'Operation Restore Trust:' Expanded Initiative Builds on Recovery Success." May 20, 1997. *http://archive.hhs.gov/news/press/1997pres/970520.html.*

9. (OIG). *Work Plan. https://oig.hhs.gov/reports-and-publications/archives/workplan/2013/Work-Plan-2013.pdf.*

10. (OIG). "Exclusion Authorities." *http://oig.hhs.gov/fraud/exclusions.asp.*

11. Association of Clinical Documentation Improvement Specialists (ACDIS). "Put PEPPER to proper use." *CDI Journal*, Vol. 5, No. 2, April 2011. *www.hcpro.com/content/264417.pdf.*

12. Cheung-Larivee, K. "AHA, hospitals sue HHS for denied outpatient Medicare payments," FierceHealthcare, November 2, 2012. *www.fiercehealthcare.com/story/aha-hospitals-sue-hhs-denied-outpatient-medicare-payments/2012-11-02#ixzz2LwkhYgZf.*

13. Centers for Medicare & Medicaid Services (CMS). "Recovery Auditing in the Medicare and Medicaid Programs for Fiscal Year 2011." *www.cms.gov/Research-Statistics-Data-and-Systems/Monitoring-Programs/Recovery-Audit-Program/Downloads/FY2011- Report-To-Congress.pdf.*

14. ACDIS. "Complex DRG audits reveal CDI target areas." *CDI Journal*, Vol. 3, No. 1. January 1, 2010. *www.hcpro.com/acdis/details. cfm?topic=WS_ACD_JNL&content_id=244318.*

15. American Hospital Association. *RACTrack.* August 2012. *www.aha.org/advocacy-issues/rac/ractrac.shtml.*

16. ACDIS. "Recovery Auditor activity increases: Prepayment review demonstration begins; CDI role in audit defense gains momentum." *CDI Journal.* October 2012, Vol. 6, No. 4. *www.hcpro.com/content/285116.pdf.*

17. ACDIS. "Is your CDI team involved in Recovery Audit reviews and/or denial management?" *CDI Poll.* April 25, 2012. *www.hcpro. com/acdis/view_readerpoll_results.cfm?quiz_id=2472.*

18. CMS. "Quality Improvement Organizations." *www.cms.gov/Medicare/Quality-Initiatives-Patient-Assessment-Instruments /QualityImprovementOrgs/index.html?redirect=/qualityimprovementorgs.*

19. CMS. "Recovery Auditing in the Medicare and Medicaid Programs for Fiscal Year 2011." *www.cms.gov/Research-Statistics-Data- and-Systems/Monitoring-Programs/Recovery-Audit-Program/Downloads/FY2011-Report-To-Congress.pdf.*

20. CMS. *www.cms.gov/Medicare/Quality-Initiatives-Patient-Assessment-Instruments/QualityImprovementOrgs/index.html?redirect= /qualityimprovementorgs.*

3 Coding Advancements

Although the International Classification of Diseases (ICD) system has been around since the late 1800s, Congress passed the Health Information Portability and Accountability Act (HIPAA) in 1996 that requires the use of specified code sets for particular types of claims to standardize all healthcare transactions. As such, the ICD code set has become the basis of the healthcare payment systems in the United States.

The current set of clinical codes, ICD, 9th Revision, clinical modification (ICD-9-CM), has been used in the United States since 1980—more than 30 years. Since its implementation, however, it became increasingly difficult to integrate new codes to accurately describe contemporary diseases, groundbreaking medical procedures, and other new technology.

So, in 2009, Centers for Medicare & Medicaid Services (CMS) announced its intent to move to the 10th Revision (ICD-10) and adapt both a clinical modification (CM) and procedure coding system (PCS) for billing and reimbursement purposes by 2013. After much debate and industry unrest, however, the U.S. Department of Health and Human Services (HHS) delayed implementation and set a new deadline for October 1, 2014.[1]

Code Specificity

ICD-9-CM contained 24,000 codes. ICD-10-CM/PCS contains more than 150,000. As one might suspect, additional codes provide additional specificity, frequently called "granularity," to describe the condition and care afforded to a given patient. Seventy-five percent of the new ICD-10 code set has a "one-to-many" code translation—meaning, one code in ICD-9-CM translates into many codes in ICD-10-CM/PCS.

For example, ICD-9-CM code 998.11, Hemorrhage complicating a procedure, equates to I97.4, Intraoperative hemorrhage and hematoma of a circulatory system organ or structure complicating a cardiac catheterization, or, depending on the specificity captured in the documentation, could map to I97.41, I97.410, I97.411, I97.418, or I97.42.[2]

FIGURE 3.1 ◇ **ICD-9-CM/ICD-10-CM CODE DIFFERENCES**

ICD-9-CM Diagnosis Codes	ICD-10-CM Diagnosis Codes
3-5 characters in length	3-7 characters in length
Approximately 13,500 codes	Approximately 69,000 available codes
First digit may be alpha (E or V) or numeric; Digits 2-5 are numeric	Digit 1 is alpha; Digits 2 and 3 are numeric; Digits 4-7 are alpha or numeric
Limited space for adding new code	Flexible for adding new codes
Lacks detail	Very specific
Lacks laterality	Has laterality
Difficult to analyze data due to non-specific codes	Specificity improves coding accuracy and richness of data for analysis
Codes are nonspecific and do not adequately define diagnoses needed for medical research	Detail improves the accuracy of data used for medical research
Does not support interoperability because it is not used by other countries	Supports interoperability and the exchange of health data between other countries and the United States

Source: The CDI Specialist's Guide to ICD-10.

FIGURE 3.2 ◇ **ICD-9/ICD-10 PROCEDURE CODE DIFFERENCES**

ICD-9-CM Procedure Codes	ICD-10-PCS Procedure Codes
3-4 numbers in length	7 alpha-numeric characters in length
Approximately 4,000 codes	Approximately 190,000 available codes
Based upon outdated technology	Reflects current usage of medical terminology and devices
Limited space for adding new codes	Flexible for adding new codes
Lacks detail	Very specific
Lacks laterality	Has laterality
Generic terms for body parts	Detailed descriptions for body parts
Lacks description of methodology and approach for procedures	Provides detailed descriptions of methodology and approach for procedures
Limits DRG assignment	Allows DRG definitions to better recognize new technologies and device
Lacks precision to adequately define procedures	Precisely defines procedures with detail regarding body part, approach, any device used, and qualifying information

Source: The CDI Specialist's Guide to ICD-10.

Figures 3.1 and 3.2 illustrate the differences in structure and format of the different coding systems.

If ICD-10-CM/PCS is used to its full potential, it will provide greater detail and a more accurate depiction of patient severity. This level of detail is expected to provide more information about the relationship between a provider's performance and the patient's condition. And this, most believe, should enhance the ability to measure quality and meet initiatives, such as value-based purchasing discussed in Chapter 1.

That means facilities will need more specific documentation to capture the right code. It will also mean that it could take longer to code and to obtain the necessary documentation. Considering current difficulties related to capturing the clinical information needed for coding, the increased need for CDI assistance could increase as exponentially as the code set itself.

Physician queries as ICD-10 training tools

Many facilities plan to employ CDI specialists as frontline educators for physician ICD-10 documentation training. Any number of training tactics may prove successful. In fact, employing a multidisciplined approach incorporating ICD-10 documentation tips into physician newsletters, presenting targeted education during short PowerPoint presentations, and crafting ICD-9 to ICD-10 crosswalk tip sheets all are viable options.[3]

Many facilities have already begun to train staff (sometimes covertly) using their query forms. To do this, review current documentation trends of your facility's top 10 to 20 MS-DRGs and review against new ICD-10 documentation requirements. Identify areas for improvement and begin to incorporate these elements into existing physician queries and educational presentations.[4]

For example, at one Long Island, N.Y., facility, a few focus areas included:

- **Myocardial infarction (MI):** In ICD-10, documentation of MI requires both a location of the MI as well as whether the MI is an embolus or a thrombus (provided that a cardiac catheter has been performed). To prepare for this change, ensure that queries refer to any MI documentation that exists in the record as well as any lab or other imaging findings emphasizing the cause-and-effect relationship of the MI to any documented blockage in the cath report and focusing on capturing where the occlusion took place.

- **Cerebrovascular accidents (CVA):** CDI specialists should also ask physicians to document the site of the occlusion (e.g., the pons) for all CVA cases in preparation for ICD-10. Note that this level of specificity does not impede coding in ICD-9, as these cases are ultimately still coded as a basic infarction or bleed.

- Surgical procedures: ICD-10 requires more specificity in identifying muscles involved in surgical procedures, as well as femoral popliteal bypass surgeries, angiographies, and more. Work closely with vascular surgeons to discuss the changes and ensure documentation in dictated operative reports.[5]

Figure 3.3 illustrates one possible example of an ICD-10 query form related to cerebral infarction.

If physicians already have difficulty fully documenting patient acuity for MS-DRGs, then evaluating the quality of physician documentation and assessing the need for physician education and practical training should be an immediate priority. An assessment of the top diagnosis and/or product lines can help prioritize documentation improvement efforts. Determine how many "unspecified" ICD-9 codes—such as 285.9, Anemia, unspecified; 414.00, Coronary artery disease of unspecified type of vessel; or 428.0, Congestive heart failure, unspecified—the facility already reports and then target queries in these areas for additional specificity.

Other query and educational efforts can be identified by analyzing the difference in the number of codes in ICD-9 and in ICD-10 by product line and high-volume services. For example, product lines with more procedure codes might be more likely to require more specific documentation related to anatomy, device, etc. CDI specialists can conduct a targeted set of reviews for specific procedures to identify documentation improvement opportunities. Note that poor documentation for high-volume services can represent potential risk once the ICD-10 code set is in place.

In advance of ICD-10 implementation, CDI programs need to review their query policies and procedures to ensure compliance and assess/reassess CDI program successes. Use CDI policies and procedures as a starting point for audits and other reviews. Effective audits will illustrate trends, such as whether

FIGURE 3.3 ◇ **SAMPLE ICD-10-CM QUERY FOR CEREBRAL INFARCTION**

Date: _____

Dear Treating Medical Team

Patient demographic information

bar code for scanning

Please clarify the following information related to the diagnosis of "cerebral infarction" that appears in the History and Physical:

1. What type of event caused the "cerebral infarction"?
    a. Embolism
    b. Thrombosis
    c. Occlusion/Stenosis
    d. Unable to determine
    e. Other _____

2. What is the location of the "cerebral infarction"?
    a. Vertebral artery
        • Right   • Left
    b. Carotid artery
        • Right   • Left
    c. Middle cerebral artery
        • Right   • Left
    d. Anterior cerebral artery
        • Right   • Left
    e. Posterior cerebral artery
        • Right   • Left
    f. Cerebellar artery
        • Right   • Left
    g. Unable to determine
    h. other _____

If you have any questions, please feel free to contact me: CDI @ ext. 2-2222

Provider authentication:

_____

Date   Time   Print name   Sign name   credentials

Please be advised this document is a part of the permanent medical record

Source: The Clinical Documentation Improvement Specialist's Guide to ICD-10, Second Edition.

records are being reviewed in a timely manner, whether clinical indicators were captured on the query form, and whether the query language was leading or otherwise inappropriate.[6]

Incorporating Coding Guidelines

Through a written memorandum of understanding between the American Hospital Association (AHA) and the National Center for Health Statistics (NCHS) in 1963, the AHA Central Office was established as a clearinghouse for issues related to ICD-9-CM use. The Central Office works with the other cooperating parties to maintain the integrity of the ICD-9-CM classification system, recommending revisions and modifications as it develops educational material and programs. The cooperating parties include:

- AHA

- American Health Information Management Association (AHIMA)

- CMS

- NHCS

The same process will apply to ICD-10. Although the codes are traditionally updated annually, a "code freeze" was put into place until the ICD-10 implementation date in order to ease the transition.

Similarly, just as the *Official Guidelines for Coding and Reporting* governs code assignment in ICD-9, the same holds true for ICD-10.[7]

Despite numerous changes to the code set, most of the *Official Guidelines for Coding and Reporting* remains the same in ICD-10. Of particular importance to note, in terms of understanding the impetus for a physician query, is governance regarding code sequencing or how certain conditions must be reported in a certain order—namely, the principal diagnosis followed by additional or secondary diagnoses.

Principal diagnosis

Overall, assigning the principal diagnosis is probably the most difficult aspect of determining the correct Medicare severity diagnosis-related group (MS-DRG) assignment. Acute care hospitals use the Uniform

Hospital Discharge Data Set (UHDDS) definitions to report inpatient data elements in a standardized manner. UHDDS defines the principal diagnosis as:

The condition established after careful study to be chiefly responsible for occasioning the admission of the patient to the hospital for care.[8]

However, healthcare providers may not always identify the principal diagnosis at the time of admission. For example, a patient admitted with abdominal pain due to an intestinal obstruction may have a primary diagnosis of small bowel cancer that is diagnosed after further testing and analysis. When the principal diagnosis is unclear, ambiguous, or conflicting, a physician query is not only necessary but mandatory.

The circumstances of the inpatient (not necessarily the outpatient or observation) admission, the diagnostic approach, and the treatment rendered factor heavily in its determination. Once a principal diagnosis is determined, additional codes are sequenced according to guidance from:

- Coding conventions in ICD-9-CM, volumes 1 and 2 (soon to be ICD-10-CM/PCS)

- *Official Guidelines for Coding and Reporting*

- Advice rendered by the AHA's *Coding Clinic*

To capture the resources that the hospital consumes during the workup process, the physician needs to document all the diagnoses that he or she believes may cause the patient's symptoms. That means that, in the inpatient setting, the physician needs to document all probable, possible, presumed, and/or suspected diagnoses and empiric treatments. The *Official Guidelines for Coding and Reporting* allow for coding of uncertain diagnoses as long as they are documented at the time of discharge. This guideline differs from outpatient/physician coding guidelines, so it may prove to be a point of confusion for clinical and physician staff members.

Consider the following symptoms and their corresponding differential diagnoses:

- Chest pain (symptom): Unstable angina, coronary artery disease, atherosclerotic disease, peptic ulcer disease (differential diagnoses)

- Syncope (symptom): Arrhythmia, cerebrovascular accident (CVA), electrolyte imbalance, dehydration (differential diagnoses)

- Altered mental status (symptom): Transient ischemic attack, sepsis, CVA, intracranial bleed (differential diagnoses)

- Shortness of breath (symptom): Pulmonary embolism, exacerbation of chronic obstructive pulmonary disease, acute exacerbation of diastolic heart failure (differential diagnoses)

As a general rule, when the physician determines a more definitive diagnosis, this more concrete diagnosis becomes the principal diagnosis.

Secondary diagnosis

MS-DRGs require clear and consistent documentation of all conditions treated during the patient's hospital stay. Additional and secondary diagnoses should be reported when they affect patient care in regard to the following:

- Clinical evaluation

- Therapeutic treatment

- Diagnostic procedures

- Extended length of hospital stay

- Increased nursing care and monitoring[9]

Additional diagnoses are defined as:

> *All conditions that coexist at the time of admission, that develop subsequently, or that affect the treatment received and/or the length of stay. Diagnoses that relate to an earlier episode which have no bearing on the current hospital stay are to be excluded.*[10]

These are times when sequencing the diagnoses becomes important to ensure an accurate reflection of severity of illness and, as ICD-10-CM/PCS implementation takes place, this will become extremely important for accurate code assignment. CDI specialists need to educate providers on the need to specify the acuity of all conditions and to:

- Determine whether the condition is a new condition (acute)

- Document time of onset

- Determine if the admission meets medical necessity

- Assess whether the condition is a chronic condition that has worsened (exacerbation)

- Identify medical record documentation identifying how the patient differs from usual/baseline functioning[11]

Figure 3.4 illustrates possible query options for capturing the acuity of a diagnosis—in this instance, the query aims to capture whether the gastritis is a new condition or exacerbation of an existing condition.

The ICD-10-CM/PCS code set contains many more guidelines for sequencing, such as additional "includes" and "excludes" notes which indicate when two diagnoses can and cannot be coded together; the use of combination codes in situations where one code clearly identifies all the elements documented in the diagnosis; and paired codes for etiology/manifestation of diagnoses. All these considerations will soon fall within the scope of CDI practices as program staff prepare for ICD-10-CM/PCS implementation.[12]

Additionally, CDI specialists will need to query in situations where clinical indicators in the record seem to point to one condition caused by or due to another condition. These "cause-and-effect" clarifications may best be clarified by "yes/no" queries as illustrated in Figure 3.5.

FIGURE 3.4 ◇ SAMPLE ICD-10-CM ACUITY QUERY

The diagnosis "gastritis" appears in the history and physical. Please clarify the patient's disease process in your next progress note or the discharge summary by stating if the gastritis is . . .

❏ New onset/acute
❏ Chronic
❏ Exacerbation/worsening of a chronic condition
❏ Unable to determine
❏ Other: _____

Source: The Clinical Documentation Improvement Specialist's Guide to ICD-10, Second Edition.

ICD-9-CM resources

The AHA Central Office administers coding advice via *Coding Clinic for ICD-9-CM* for individual circumstances submitted by the general public, including questions regarding physician queries on scenarios concerning ICD-9-CM. It is deemed by most coding professionals and regulators as official advice. Case situations published in the AHA's *Coding Clinic for ICD-9-CM* can be used to support code assignment when challenged by outside entities, such as Recovery Auditors or fiscal intermediaries. Likewise, Recovery Auditors or other agents can cite *Coding Clinic for ICD-9-CM* when challenging code or DRG assignments made by providers.

Note, guidance from *Coding Clinic for ICD-9-CM* will not be applicable once ICD-10-CM/PCS implementation takes place. Previous guidance will also not be translated into ICD-10-CM/PCS. However, AHA began accepting questions related to ICD-10 in its Fourth Quarter 2012 edition.[13]

Although most expect the AHA to continue to provide such insight as the nation moves closer and closer to ICD-10-CM/PCS implementation, the Fourth Quarter 2012 information did not address big issues such as defining chronic conditions (i.e., COPD, diabetes, obesity), so they are considered reportable/ always clinically significant in the inpatient setting regardless of the "absence of documented intervention or further evaluation" (see *Coding Clinic* Third Quarter 2011, p. 4, and Third Quarter 2007, pp. 13–14). Nor does it address whether the term "acute exacerbation of a chronic condition (heart failure)" can be considered as acute-on-chronic (see First Quarter 2009, p. 7), for example.[14]

It did offer guidance on the following topics:

- Acute exacerbation of asthma and status asthmaticus

- Sequencing of acute MI with subsequent infarction

- Rib resection with reconstruction of anterior chest wall

- Crohn's disease with rectal abscess

- Initial encounter for fracture malunion

FIGURE 3.5 ◇ SAMPLE YES/NO QUERIES FOR CLARIFICATION

Compliant Example 1

Clinical Scenario: A patient is admitted with cellulitis around a recent operative wound site, and only cellulitis is documented without any relationship to the recent surgical procedure.

Query: Is the cellulitis due to or the result of the surgical procedure? Please document your response in the health record or below.

Yes _____
No _____
Other _____
Clinically Undetermined _____
Name: _____ Date: _____

Rationale: This is an example of a yes/no query involving a documented condition potentially resulting from a procedure.

Compliant Example 2

Clinical scenario: Congestive heart failure is documented in the final discharge statement in a patient who is noted to have an echocardiographic interpretation of systolic dysfunction and is maintained on lisinopril, Lasix, and Lanoxin.

Query: Based on the echocardiographic interpretation of systolic dysfunction in this patient maintained on lisinopril, Lasix, and Lanoxin can your documentation of "congestive heart failure" be further specified as <u>systolic congestive heart failure</u>? Please document your response in the health record or below.

Yes _____
No _____
Other _____
Clinically Undetermined _____
Name: _____ Date: _____

Rationale: This yes/no query provides an example of determining the specificity of a condition that is documented as an interpretation of an echocardiogram.

Source: Guidelines for Achieving a Compliant Query Practice.

Additional Query Opportunities

Both the *Official Guidelines for Coding and Reporting* and the *Coding Clinic for ICD-9-CM* articulate many cases whereby querying is strongly suggested, if not mandatory. Failure to query as an error of omission is just as serious as inappropriate or poorly worded queries. The appendix of this book lists the areas of ICD-9-CM that address query opportunities as well as *Coding Clinic* articles that cite the importance of physician queries.

REFERENCES

1. Association of Clinical Documentation Improvement Specialists (ACDIS). "ICD-10 Deadline: Implementation date set at October 1, 2014." *CDI Journal*, Vol. 6, No. 4, October 2012. *www.hcpro.com/content/285104.pdf*. Accessed February 2013.

2 Avery J., Ericson C. *The CDI Specialist's Guide to ICD-10*, Second Edition. ACDIS. May 2013. Danvers, Mass. HCPro, Inc.

3. ACDIS. "Suggested ICD-10 Implementation Timeline." *CDI Journal*, Vol. 6, No. 4, October 2012. *www.hcpro.com/content/285104 .pdf*. Accessed February 2013.

4. Krauss G., Hoffman S. *The CDI Specialist's Guide to ICD-10*, First Edition. ACDIS. March 2011. Danvers, Mass.: HCPro, Inc.

5. Ibid.

6. ACDIS. "Conduct peer audits to provide query practice insight." *CDI Journal*, Vol. 7, No. 1. January 2013. *www.hcpro.com /content/288079.pdf*. Accessed February 2013.

7. Centers for Disease Control. Official Guidelines for Coding and Reporting. *www.cdc.gov/nchs/data/icd9/icdguide10.pdf*.

8. Uniform Hospital Discharge Data Set.

9. Ibid.

10. Ibid.

11. Ericson, C. "ICD-10 for CDI Boot Camp." 2013, Danvers, Mass: HCPro Inc. *www.hcprobootcamps.com/courses/10051/overview*.

12. Avery J., Ericson C. *The CDI Specialist's Guide to ICD-10*, Second Edition. ACDIS. May 2013. Danvers, Mass.: HCPro, Inc.

13. Ericson C. "Recap of Fourth Quarter Coding Clinic." *CDI Journal*, Vol. 7, No. 1. January 2013. *www.hcpro.com/content/288079.pdf*. Accessed February 2013.

14. Ibid.

Progression of Query Guidance

Why are physician queries so critical to accurate documentation and coding? The answer can be found in the *Official Guidelines for Coding and Reporting*, which states:

> *A joint effort between the health care provider and the coding professional is essential to achieve complete and accurate documentation, code assignment, and reporting of diagnoses and procedures. The importance of consistent, complete documentation in the medical record cannot be overemphasized.*[1]

Note that the same statement remains in the latest draft of the International Classification of Diseases, 10th Revision (ICD-10) guidelines. As previously discussed, lack of accurate and complete documentation results in nonspecific coding. This, in turn, influences data integrity and reimbursement and presents potential compliance risks. These rules emphasize the role of communication throughout the process.

The *Official Guidelines for Coding and Reporting* expects physician participation in this endeavor. Accurate documentation is not a one-way street, despite any pushback clinicians and coders may experience from physicians. Although some may find it difficult to believe, physicians are required to write legibly, clearly, and with precision and reliably.

Supporting these goals are requirements from The Joint Commission, an independent, not-for-profit organization that accredits and certifies more than 20,000 healthcare organizations and programs in the United States. It emphasizes that facilities and physicians must ensure that:

- The medical record contains sufficient information to:

  - Identify the patient

  - Support the diagnosis/condition

  - Justify the care, treatment, and services

– Document the course and results of care, treatments, and services

– Promote continuity of care among providers

- The review of medical records is based on hospital-defined indicators that address:

    – The presence

    – Timeliness

    – Readability (whether handwritten or printed)

    – Quality

    – Consistency

    – Clarity

    – Accuracy

    – Completeness

    – Authentication of data and information contained within the record

- A concise discharge summary provides information to other caregivers and facilitates continuity of care, including:

    – The reason for hospitalization

    – Significant findings

    – Procedures performed and care, treatment, and services provided

    – The patient's condition at discharge

    – Information provided to the patient and family, as appropriate

- The hospital defines a complete record and the time frame within which the record is completed after discharge, not to exceed 30 days after discharge[2]

Medicare's *Conditions of Participation* likewise support appropriate physician documentation by stating the following requirements:

- All entries must be legible and complete and must be authenticated and dated promptly by the person (identified by name and discipline) who is responsible for ordering, providing, or evaluating the service furnished

- All records must show documentation of complications, hospital-acquired infections, and unfavorable reactions to drugs and anesthesia[3]

All this ultimately leads to the importance of appropriate physician documentation and the translation of that documentation into usable data. Given that most physicians have minimal medical coding training and awareness of Centers for Medicare & Medicaid Services (CMS) payment methods and fraud and abuse risks, clinical documentation improvement (CDI) specialists and coders have an enormous responsibility to help ensure the documentation physicians provide best represents the codes that match the diagnoses and care provided.

The question quickly becomes how to help physicians understand the importance of their documentation and its inherent worth—namely, that improved documentation equals improved healthcare.

Enter CDI efforts and physician queries.

Government Query Guidance

Following the hubbub of Medicare severity diagnosis-related group (MS-DRG) implementation and related documentation and coding adjustment payment decreases, facilities worried how they would be able to capture potentially at-risk reimbursement. To answer those fears (as indicated in earlier in the book), the 2008 inpatient prospective payment system (IPPS) final rule included the following instruction:

> *We do not believe there is anything inappropriate, unethical or otherwise wrong with hospitals taking full advantage of coding opportunities to maximize Medicare payment that is supported by documentation in the medical record.*[4]

The statement lent credence to the previous practice of both concurrent CDI and retrospective coder-initiated physician queries and opened the proverbial floodgates for renewed efforts in concurrent record review and queries.

Given the U.S. Department of Health and Human Services' (HHS) concerns regarding the risks of physician query efforts (as described in Chapters 1 and 2), one would expect that HHS, via the CMS or other government agency, would generate rules regarding the query process.

In fact, CMS has shed little light on the matter since 2001, when it stated in a memorandum to its Quality Improvement Organizations (QIO) that:

> *Use of the physician query form is permissible to the extent that it provides clarification and is consistent with other medical record documentation.*[5]

In the memorandum, CMS further instructs QIOs to refer cases to a QIO physician reviewer for evaluation if the physician query:

- Is leading in nature

- Introduces new information

QIO medical directors still maintain authority to determine the legality of a physician query.

> *In conducting medical review for validating the DRG, the reviewer shall use his or her professional judgment and discretion in considering the information contained on a physician query form along with the rest of the medical record. If the physician query form is leading in nature or if it introduces new information, the case shall be referred to a physician for further review.*[6]

Determining how organizations actually carry out the query process, however, was something the government left to industry organizations and the healthcare entities themselves.

American Health Information Management Association (AHIMA) Input

Historically, health information management (HIM) staff members/coders have performed retrospective (postdischarge) queries to ensure the specificity and completeness of data. As one of the largest

HIM associations, and as one of the four cooperating parties governing the maintenance of the U.S. adaptation of the International Classification of Diseases (ICD) code sets, any advice from AHIMA bears additional weight, carrying with it as it does the moniker of "industry best practice."

AHIMA could be seen to support physician query efforts in its "Code of Ethics," when it stated that members must facilitate "interdisciplinary collaboration" in situations "supporting HIM functions"— namely, interpreting the medical record and asking physicians for additional information necessary to appropriately assign codes.[7]

It wasn't until 2001, however, that AHIMA published its first query practice brief, "Developing a Physician Query Process," thus creating the industry standard from which facilities could base their own query policies and procedures. In it, AHIMA outlined documentation expectations of both physicians and coders, identified possible query formats, and provided definitions to help describe leading queries.[8]

Standards

In 2008, AHIMA crafted its "Standards of Ethical Coding," which further delineated coding and querying activities. It states that HIM/coding professionals can assign only:

> *Codes and data that are clearly and consistently supported by health record documentation in accordance with applicable code set and abstraction conventions, rules, and guidelines.*[9]

When such information is missing, the "Standards" direct coders to:

> *Query the provider for clarification and additional documentation prior to code assignment.*

Specifically, it requires that coders query the physician when "information regarding a significant reportable condition, procedure, or other reportable data element (e.g., a present-on-admission [POA] indicator) is:

- Conflicting

- Incomplete

- Ambiguous

In Article 4 of the "Standards," AHIMA calls on HIM/coding professionals to:

- "Participate in the development of query policies that support documentation improvement and meet regulatory, legal, and ethical standards for coding and reporting

- Query the provider for clarification when documentation in the health record that affects an externally reportable data element is illegible, incomplete, unclear, inconsistent, or imprecise

- Use queries as a communication tool to improve the accuracy of code assignment and the quality of health record documentation . . . not to inappropriately increase reimbursement or misrepresent quality of care"

Of particular note, AHIMA's "Standards" explicitly state that coding professionals should not query the provider if clinical evidence regarding the diagnosis does not exists, citing the example of querying a provider for the presence of gram-negative pneumonia on every pneumonia case regardless of other indicators in the medical record.[10]

Many experts felt the "Standards" did not go far enough toward ensuring compliant practices, and many worried that with the expansion of CDI programs staffed by clinical rather than coding professionals, adherence to the "Standards" could be lax.

'Managing an Effective Query Process'

Consequently, AHIMA conferred a committee to redraft its 2001 query brief, published a tentative document on May 12, 2008, titled "Queries as a Tool for Clinical Documentation Improvement," and opened it up to public comment. Numerous healthcare parties provided feedback and worked with AHIMA on its final guidance, "Managing an Effective Query Process," released that October.[11]

In it, AHIMA listed the following nonexclusive circumstances and examples for which physician queries are appropriate:

- Illegibility: defined as handwriting that cannot be read by two other individuals.

- Incompleteness: can be represented by an abnormal test result for which a clinical interpretation has not been given or the indication for a prescribed pharmaceutical was not provided.

 Physician Queries Handbook, Second Edition

- Lack of clarity: can be represented by a patient with a symptom for which an underlying cause was not elucidated (e.g., fever, abdominal pain).

- Inconsistency: represented by conflicting documentation by a treating provider (e.g., sepsis on one progress note, urosepsis on the discharge summary) or between two different providers (e.g., stroke documented by a neurologist, transient ischemic attack documented by the attending physician on the discharge summary).

- Imprecision: represented by the need for greater specificity of diagnoses when allowed for by ICD-9-CM. For example, fourth- and fifth-digit codes for CHF characterize it as acute or chronic systolic or diastolic failure in ICD-9-CM.

Similar to previous statements, this brief limits queries to situations where the documentation is conflicting, ambiguous, or incomplete and reiterated that those submitting queries should not direct the physician to any particular diagnosis nor indicate any financial or quality reporting outcomes as a result of any potential answer the physician might provide.

In keeping with the theme of asking unbiased questions of the physician, the brief offered additional specifics about various query types, stating that handwritten sticky notes, scratch paper, or other notes that could be easily removed and discarded are not permissible. The informal nature of such notes, the thinking goes, may make them easy for physicians to ignore and possibly make it even easier for anyone to throw away after the fact, making it impossible to determine if the query was leading to begin with.

Instead, the 2008 brief states:

> *The preferred formats for capturing the query include facility-approved query form, facsimile transmission, electronic communication on secure e-mail, or secure IT messaging system.*[12]

It offered some concrete guidance on how CDI specialists and coders should query physicians through the use of forms and defined how forms should be created. Checklists of possible diagnoses are permissible, it said, provided the form contains options for "unable to determine" and "other." Simpler, "yes/no" questions, it said, were not permissible, except in determining whether the condition was POA. Although the brief acknowledged growing use of verbal queries, it made no other recommendation other than following nonleading, unbiased practices.

To protect the integrity of the query process, the brief recommended regular auditing for efficiency, rates of query responses, and compliance to ensure that staff members avoid excessive querying and leading submissions.

The brief pointed to the fact that, because coders ultimately hold responsibility for assigning the final DRG, the HIM department should be established as "owners" of the physician query process despite the fact that many CDI programs were housed within case management or quality departments at the time.[13]

CDI-specific recommendations

The outpouring of input regarding the 2008 practice brief spurred AHIMA to convene a 30-member committee the following year. More than 100 volunteers applied for the workgroup effort. AHIMA initially hoped to compile the volunteers' research into a large volume or book, but volunteers were adamant that the results be provided openly and freely.[14]

So, in the spring of 2010, just two years after the publication of "Managing an Effective Query Process," AHIMA convened a comprehensive committee to draft "Guidance for Clinical Documentation Improvement Programs," in the *Journal of AHIMA*.[15] It also published a 41-page *Clinical Documentation Improvement Toolkit*[16] and, in the fall of that same year, the *Ethical Standards for Clinical Documentation Improvement Professionals*.[17]

Much of the 2010 guidance and toolkit contents echoed previously held query best practices regarding CDI program structure, staffing, and query policies and complimented AHIMA's previous query guidance. Unlike the 2008 guidance, however, the 2010 submission acknowledged that programs are frequently housed under either the HIM or case management umbrella and that such cases are typically reported up through the finance department. It also acknowledges that CDI specialists commonly come from nursing backgrounds but reiterated that anyone with appropriate clinical, coding, and regulatory knowledge may excel in the role.

It also more definitively addressed the issues of leading versus nonleading queries, offered a checklist for conducting compliant written and verbal queries, and acknowledged the important role the verbal query process plays.

"It is easy to cross that line into potentially leading the physician to a particular diagnosis when you are in the hallway having a conversation," said Kathy DeVault, RHIA, CCS, manager of professional practice resources at AHIMA in Chicago, at the time [18].

PROGRESSION OF QUERY GUIDANCE

In regard to verbal queries, the 2010 practice brief called on facilities to create policies governing:

- When verbal queries are appropriate

- Ongoing training and assessment of CDI staff to ensure compliance

- Monitoring of verbal query efforts

According to the 2010 guidance:

The advantage of a verbal query is the [CDI specialist's] ability to interact with the provider to facilitate [an] understanding of the issues that need to be addressed. However, caution must be used to ensure that the provider is allowed to make his or her own conclusions regarding the appropriateness of a particular diagnosis or service.[19]

CREATE A VERBAL QUERY POLICY

Verbal queries, in particular, have remained a source of contention for hospitals simply because they are difficult to audit and monitor. Coders and CDI specialists know that they are not supposed to lead physicians to a diagnosis, yet when questions are posed verbally, there is a significant risk that this will take place during course of conversation meant to clarify documentation. Hospitals need to specify—in their policies and procedures—why a coder or CDI specialist will initiate a verbal query as well as what the content of that verbal query will include. Consider adding the following language:

The CDI specialist may have a discussion about a patient with a physician. This discussion will be an opportunity to educate the physician and to obtain specificity in the documentation. The CDI specialist may discuss the clinical findings and documentation with the physicians involved in the care of the patient. The role of the CDI specialist is to educate the physician on the specificity of verbiage which can result in improved capture of severity of illness. In addition, the CDI specialist will pose verbal queries (questions) to the physicians so that clarification may be documented.

Source: Eramo, L. "Verbal Queries: Let Your Policy and Procedure Do the Talking," *HealthLeaders Media,* June 4, 2009.

Additional considerations regarding documenting verbal query interactions, tracking and auditing those interactions should also be included in the CDI program's policies and procedures which will be discussed further in Chapter 5.

The toolkit portion provided job descriptions, audit tools, sample queries, metrics, and analysis examples, as well as tips for how to start and maintain effective CDI program efforts.[20]

With the releases, AHIMA aimed to create solid guidelines for the CDI profession, adding further specificity to the gray area of how to conduct physician queries. The guidelines needed to be specific enough to be useful but broad enough to allow facilities to make necessary adaptations. Although the agency guidance does carry industry weight, AHIMA stated repeatedly that such recommendations should not be misconstrued as law or government regulation but as "guiding principles to implement the query process while in no way prescribing what must be done".[21]

Ethical standards

Released in November 2010, the *Ethical Standards for Clinical Documentation Improvement Professionals* were "intended to assist in decision-making processes and actions, outline expectations for making ethical decisions in the workplace, and [to] demonstrate the [CDI] professionals' commitment to integrity" [22].

The ethical standards contain nine elements, each with component parts.

The first element states that CDI programs/specialists should "facilitate accurate, complete, and consistent clinical documentation within the health record to support coding and reporting of high-quality healthcare data."

The second element states that CDI programs/specialists should "support the reporting of all healthcare data elements . . . required for external reporting purposes . . . completely and accurately, in accordance with regulatory and documentation standards and requirements and applicable official coding conventions, rules, and guidelines."

And the third element reiterates earlier query directives.

The fourth element, however, addresses a frequent CDI program problem area—the question of financial implications associated with query efforts. This guidance indicates that CDI and coding staff should:

> *Refuse to participate in or support documentation practices intended to inappropriately increase payment, qualify for insurance policy coverage, or distort data by means that do not comply with federal and state statutes, regulations, and official rules and guidelines.*

AHIMA hoped the ethical standards would serve as supportive documentation to combat the unethical or dubious pressures that CDI specialists often face—the physician who simply asks to be told what to document, the chief financial officer who ties program achievement to constant improvement in the case mix index, and the consultant who suggests that all pneumonia queries also include options for sepsis and/or septic shock.

On the surface, these seem like ordinary and perhaps simple directives. However, each holds potential compliance problems and ethical implications if applied over time.

The fifth element addressed the interdisciplinary nature of CDI and the supportive role it plays to HIM and coding departments. The ethical standards were said to apply to all CDI professionals regardless of whether they are AHIMA members or not. Such inclusionary language was meant to bring an end to the debate over the dual role some said CDI specialists perform. Some believed if nurses performed the role, they could still be considered part of the clinical care team, whereas others argued that once nurses became CDI specialists, they had to leave their bedside nursing instincts behind in favor of the rules that govern HIM and the healthcare revenue cycle.[23]

Over time, that hierarchical split melded. Today, it is generally accepted that when CDI specialists (regardless of whether they hail from nursing or coding backgrounds) think about the medical record, they must consider it clinically and investigatively and yet have a firm understanding of the rules governing code assignment without taking either impulse too far.

Elements six through nine reflect more general guidance for behaviors, such as the directive to "advance professional knowledge through continuing education" and to "protect the confidentiality of the health record at all times."

These final considerations mirror items AHIMA included in its *Code of Ethics* for its members as well as its broader *Standards for Ethical Coding*.

Input From CDI Professionals

In October 2007, HCPro, Inc., launched the first national association dedicated to the advancement of the CDI profession—the Association for Clinical Documentation Improvement Specialists (ACDIS). ACDIS gathered a 12-member advisory board comprised of coders, nurses, and physicians working in the documentation improvement field. By early 2008, ACDIS drafted a *Code of Ethics* of its own that drew heavily on ethics guidance from AHIMA and the American Association of Professional Coders.[24]

ACDIS' *Code of Ethics* stated that CDI specialists should:

> *Put service and the health and welfare of persons before self-interest, and conduct themselves in the practice of the profession so as to bring honor to themselves, their peers, and to the [CDI] profession.*[25]

Beginning with the 2008 physician query guidance, ACDIS representatives participated in each of the AHIMA query practice brief publications with multiple representatives volunteering on the various committees and the ACDIS advisory board and administration publicly endorsing AHIMA's efforts. Further, ACDIS produced multiple benchmarking surveys to provide analysis of the ongoing evolution of the profession and to provide additional resources for CDI best practices. (The 2013 physician query benchmarking data, as well as previous query benchmarking reports, are available in the downloads section of this book.)

In December 2010, the "Physician Query Benchmarking Report" illustrated that almost all of the nearly 400 respondents performed concurrent queries; half also performed retrospective queries. Of those who use query templates, 54% said they used ACDIS or AHIMA guidance to construct them. The second-highest number of respondents (roughly 45%) said they used consultants as their source for template information.

Despite the weight of AHIMA recommendations, 46% of respondents indicated that their CDI and HIM departments had separate query policies, only partially incorporated AHIMA's recommendations, dismissed AHIMA recommendations in favor of their own facility policies, or simply did not know about the AHIMA guidance.[26]

Joint ACDIS/AHIMA Guidance

In 2012, AHIMA and ACDIS announced a plan to publish a joint query practice brief. The final result of this collaboration, "Guidelines for Achieving a Compliant Query Practice," was published in the *Journal of AHIMA* in February 2013 and in the *CDI Journal* in April 2013. The document further expands previously published advice and sometimes supersedes it. Because it was officially a joint publication, it cemented the applicability of the guidance to both CDI and coding/HIM staff members [27].

Although the reasons to query remain the same, the brief focused on leading queries. Its opening lines state:

> In court an attorney can't "lead" a witness into a statement. In hospitals, coders and [CDI] specialists can't lead healthcare providers with queries. Therefore, appropriate etiquette must be followed when querying providers for additional health record information.[28]

The concept of leading queries is discussed further in Chapter 5, but, theoretically speaking, coders and CDI professionals are not physicians and therefore cannot diagnosis a patient. No matter how many clinical indicators the patient's record may contain, the physician must document the diagnosis (even if it is a possible one) in the medical record in order for the coder to code it. Asking a physician to document a particular diagnosis may lead not only to compliance risks, such as upcoding or DRG creep, but could lead to clinical confusion later on.

To avoid leading queries, the 2013 guidance identifies different query formats:

- Open-ended

- Multiple choice

- Yes-or-no

- Verbal

However, all queries must be accompanied by relevant clinical indicators to avoid any potential of leading the provider to an expected outcome. Bluntly, the latest query practice brief states that leading queries are not acceptable.

Unlike previous advice, the latest query guidance also recommends that facilities develop internal policies regarding query retention. Increasingly, Recovery Auditors request query forms as part of their medical record reviews. Although CMS remains relatively mute on the topic, its agents did state during an April 2010 "Nationwide RAC 101 Calls" that Recovery Auditors may request any documentation "they feel is necessary to conduct the review." However, "if you don't believe the physician query helps to support the claim that was billed, then you don't need to submit it," the agent said.[29]

The 2013 ACDIS/AHIMA physician query guidelines state:

> *Auditors may request copies of any queries in order to validate query wording, even if they are not considered part of the legal health record.*[30]

Many attorneys will say "they can ask for anything they want, the question is whether we legally need to supply it." As with many things in CDI, there is no definitive answer at the time this book was written. Facilities are encouraged to work with their general council to determine the best approach.[31]

The 2013 practice brief states:

> *Organizational policies should specifically address query retention ... and indicate if the query is part of the patient's permanent health record or stored as a separate business record. If the query form is not part of the health record, the policy should specify where it will be filed and the length of time it will be retained. It may be necessary to retain the query indefinitely if it contains information not documented in the health record. Auditors may request copies of any queries in order to validate query wording, even if they are not considered part of the legal health record.*[32]

Remember, if your program allows the physician to answer concurrent queries on the query forms, they must also include the terminology in future notes to ensure there is not conflicting documentation in the medical record. If the query is issued postdischarge, any addendum to the medical record must follow Joint Commission regulation and AHIMA guidelines.

Some method of query recording or retention is required to ensure the ability to collect data for trend analysis, process improvement, and educational efforts. Additional information regarding auditing and monitoring of CDI efforts is discussed later in this book.

Finally, the latest query practice guidance includes advice on introducing new diagnoses and how to identify "possible" as a qualifier for diagnosis in queries. It clarifies that the American Hospital Association's *Coding Clinic for ICD-9-CM* is informational in nature and "not an authoritative source for establishing the clinical indicators of a given diagnosis." Rather, any clinical indicators included in the query should come from the medical record and be based on consensus views of the facility's medical staff.

Ongoing Developments

The information provided by AHIMA and other organizations should be cited and incorporated into facility CDI policies and procedures. Programs should regularly audit their CDI program efforts to ensure their policies and procedures are being followed and correctly applied. Furthermore, programmatic developments should not be limited by information previously set forth by any one organization. Compliant activities should take into account various healthcare developments and ongoing clinical and regulatory changes.

That said, facilities opting to deviate from the AHIMA brief may wish to have their policies reviewed and approved by legal counsel for compliance to applicable laws and their current interpretations by regulatory authorities and courts.

REFERENCES

1. Centers for Disease Control. *Official Guidelines for Coding and Reporting. www.cdc.gov/nchs/data/icd9/icdguide10.pdf.*

2. The Joint Commission. "Record of Care, Treatment, and Services." January 2012. *www.umdnj.edu/mdstfweb/The_Joint_Commission/Record%20of%20Care%20Treatment%20%20Services.pdf.*

3. Centers for Medicare & Medicaid Services (CMS). *Medicare Claims Processing Manual, Code of Federal Regulations*, Title 42, Section 482.24. "Conditions of Participation: Medical Records Services." *http://cfr.vlex.com/vid/482-condition-participation-record-19811382.*

4. CMS. Inpatient Prospective Payment System Final Rule. *www.cms.hhs.gov/AcuteInpatientPPS/downloads/CMS-1533-FC.pdf*, p. 208.

5. Whitten J.A. "Regulatory Attention to Use of Physician Queries in Medical Records Coding." Health Care Compliance Advisor (Jones Day, April 2002). *www.jonesday.com/pubs/pubs_detail.aspx?publD=1779.* Accessed June 17, 2009.

6. CMS. *Quality Improvement Organization Manual*, Chapter 4, "Case Review." July 11, 2003. *www.cms.hhs.gov/manuals/downloads/qio110c04.pdf.*

7. American Health Information Management Association (AHIMA). "Code of Ethics." Revised October 2011. *http://library.ahima.org/xpedio/groups/public/documents/ahima/bok1_024277.hcsp?dDocName=bok1_024277.*

8. AHIMA. "Developing an Effective Physician Query Process." *Journal of AHIMA*, Vol. 72, No. 6, July 2001.

9. AHIMA House of Delegates. "AHIMA Standards of Ethical Coding." September 2008. *http://library.ahima.org/xpedio/groups/public/documents/ahima/bok2_001166.hcsp?dDocName=bok2_001166.*

10. Ibid.

11. AHIMA. "Managing an Effective Query Process." *Journal of AHIMA*, Vol. 79, No.10, October 2008. *http://library.ahima.org/xpedio/groups/public/documents/ahima/bok1_040394.hcsp?dDocName=bok1_040394.*

12. Ibid.

13. Association of Clinical Documentation Improvement Specialists (ACDIS). "AHIMA unveils final physician query brief." *CDI Journal,* Vol. 3, No. 1, January 2009. *www.hcpro.com/content/225250.pdf.*

14. ACDIS. "AHIMA releases CDI program guidance." *CDI Strategies,* May 13, 2010. *www.hcpro.com/acdis/details.cfm?topic=WS_ACD_STG&content_id=250910.*

15. AHIMA. "Guidance for Clinical Documentation Improvement Programs." *Journal of AHIMA,* Vol. 81, No. 5, May 2010. *http://library.ahima.org/xpedio/groups/public/documents/ahima/bok1_047343.hcsp?dDocName=bok1_047343.*

16. AHIMA. *The Clinical Documentation Improvement Specialists Toolkit.* Chicago: 2010.

17. AHIMA House of Delegates. "Ethical Standards for Clinical Documentation Improvement Professionals." November 2010. *http://library.ahima.org/xpedio/groups/public/documents/ahima/bok1_047842.hcsp?dDocName=bok1_047842.*

18. ACDIS. "AHIMA releases CDI program guidance." *CDI Strategies,* May 13, 2010. *www.hcpro.com/acdis/details.cfm?topic=WS_ACD_STG&content_id=250910.*

19. AHIMA. "Guidance for Clinical Documentation Improvement Programs." *Journal of AHIMA,* Vol. 81, No. 5, May 2010. *http://library.ahima.org/xpedio/groups/public/documents/ahima/bok1_047343.hcsp?dDocName=bok1_047343.*

20. AHIMA. *The Clinical Documentation Improvement Specialists Toolkit.* Chicago: 2010.

21. AHIMA House of Delegates. "Ethical Standards for Clinical Documentation Improvement Professionals." November 2010. *http://library.ahima.org/xpedio/groups/public/documents/ahima/bok1_047842.hcsp?dDocName=bok1_047842.*

22. Ibid.

23. ACDIS. "AHIMA releases ethics guidance for CDI professionals." *CDI Strategies,* November 11, 2010. *www.hcpro.com/acdis/details.cfm?topic=WS_ACD_STG&content_id=258903.*

24. ACDIS. *Code of Ethics.* January 2008. *www.hcpro.com/acdis/code_of_ethics.cfm.*

25. Ibid.

26. ACDIS. "2010 Physician Query Benchmarking Report." *CDI Journal,* Vol. 5, No. 1, January 2011. *www.hcpro.com/content/265437.pdf.*

27. AHIMA. "Guidelines for Achieving a Compliant Query Practice." *Journal of AHIMA,* Vol. 84, No. 2, February 2013. *http://library.ahima.org/xpedio/groups/public/documents/ahima/bok1_050018.hcsp?dDocName=bok1_050018.*

28. Ibid.

29. ACDIS. "RACs request queries as complex reviews roll out." *CDI Journal,* Vol. 4, No. 3, July 2010. *www.hcpro.com/content/253342.pdf.*

30. AHIMA. "Guidelines for Achieving a Compliant Query Practice." *Journal of AHIMA,* Vol. 84, No. 2, February 2013.

31. ACDIS. "RACs request queries as complex reviews roll out." *CDI Journal,* Vol. 4, No. 3, July 2010. *www.hcpro.com/content/253342.pdf.*

32. AHIMA. "Guidelines for Achieving a Compliant Query Practice." *Journal of AHIMA,* Vol. 84, No. 2, February 2013.

Redefining Query Types

Essential Query Requirements

Taking into consideration the various requirements governing the capture of healthcare data, clinical documentation improvement (CDI) programs can easily begin to itemize the basic elements needed for compliant queries.

First, as stated in almost all the American Health Information Management Association (AHIMA) industry guidance, query forms should be vetted and approved by the organization and should be tracked or documented in some manner. They should not be written on sticky notes or another slip of paper that may run the risk of being discarded or discounted.

Furthermore, because it must meet the basic tenets of information exchange, the query form should include:

- Patient name or identification number

- Admission date and/or date of service

- Health record or account number

- Date the query was initiated

- Date the query was closed

- Name and contact information of the individual initiating the query

- Name and contact information of the physician responding to the query

- Statement of the issue in the form of a question, along with clinical indicators specified from the chart

Although AHIMA does not state whether hospitals should include a disclaimer on their query forms, many choose to include language such as:

> *In responding to this query, please exercise your expert, independent judgment. The fact that a question is asked does not imply that any particular answer is desired or expected.*

Remember, however, that even the inclusion of such language may not protect the organization against claims denials, allegations of upcoding, or fraud if a pattern of submitting leading queries is identified. Nevertheless, many organizations consider inclusion of such a disclaimer an important reminder to physicians and CDI professionals that the ultimate decision regarding the patient's care lay with the provider responsible for that care.

Simple communication basics also help ensure query practice success. Always use "please" and "thank you." Avoid improper grammar and incomplete sentences. A physician may discount the veracity of the query if he/she cannot clearly identify the objective. Regardless of query format, CDI staff must ensure the query clearly and concisely identifies the clinical indicators and the relevance of the inquiry. Queries should be easy to read and easy to answer. If the physician needs to read the form more than once to understand the query, he/she will not take the time to do so.

When to Query

The primary reason for physician queries is based on the *Official Guidelines for Coding and Reporting* suggestion that a "joint effort" between the coders and providers results in the most accurate and complete documentation.[1] When documentation is unclear, a query may be necessary.

Throughout query practice advances, the reasons for queries remain relatively unchanged since the first AHIMA release in 2001. To review, reasons to query include when documentation:

- Is conflicting, imprecise, incomplete, illegible, ambiguous, or contains inconsistent information

- Describes or is associated with clinical indicators without a definitive relationship to an underlying diagnosis

- Includes clinical indicators, diagnostic evaluation, and/or treatment not related to a specific condition or procedure

- Provides a diagnosis without underlying clinical validation

- Is unclear for present-on-admission indicator assignment

For example, Figure 5.1 illustrates how these concerns might be effectively addressed in a generic query form.

FIGURE 5.1 ◇ SAMPLE GENERIC QUERY FORM

ABC MEDICAL CENTER

Documentation Clarification Request	No.
CATEGORY: Clinical Documentation Improvement Procedure	No.
TITLE: CLINICAL DOCUMENTATION CLARIFICATION REQUEST	No.

Current Revision Date: xx/xx/xx   Supersedes: N/A   Original Effective Date: xx/xx/xx   Page X of Y

Date: _____

Dear Dr. _____:

A review of the record of [insert patient identification number] identifies the need for additional clarification due to one (or more) of the following circumstances (circle all that apply):

    a)   Clinical indicators of a diagnosis but no documentation of the condition
    b)   Clinical evidence for a higher degree of specificity or severity
    c)   A cause-and-effect relationship between two conditions or organism
    d)   An underlying cause when admitted with symptoms
    e)   Only the treatment is documented (without a diagnosis documented)
    f)   Present on admission (POA indicator status)

Please provide the requested clarification in the progress notes and/or discharge summary

(Insert request here. Include clinical indicators)

Thank you for your assistance
Respectfully submitted,

_____

(insert name of CDS Reviewer)

_____

(contact information (phone/e-mail, etc.)

Source: ACDIS Forms & Tools Library.

Clinical Evidence

The easiest way to ensure that CDI specialists submit queries to physicians only when clinically appropriate is through the use of clinical indicators—a written set of guidelines based on the most current medical literature.

Historically, coders received mixed messages regarding the use of clinical evidence in their queries. On one hand, guidance (and physician staff) point out coders' lack of medical experience—they are told they are not physicians, not entitled to "practice" medicine, and that they should simply code the diagnoses written by the physician. On the other hand, various agencies and payers opine that coding a diagnosis without clinical evidence is a coding error.

When querying, avoid diagnostic indications but provide objective clinical information and documentation from the medical record, identify where in the medical record such indicators originated, and reference the documentation concern at issue. Address the document and date where the issue was found. The physician will not cooperate if he or she thinks the coder or CDI specialist is trying to practice medicine. Figure 5.2 illustrates one way a physician query might incorporate such information.

Authoritative advice

Since the AHIMA published its October 2008 guidance, "Managing an Effective Query Process," coders became empowered to ask important questions. Although coding is supposed to be black and white, the reality is that medicine, and its corresponding documentation, has many shades of gray. To contextualize that "gray," those who query physicians frequently use textbook and Web-based references to determine the clinical presentation of many diagnoses. Such literature helps the CDI specialist determine when a clinical picture, as described in the medical record, is indicative of a particular diagnosis. Standard peer-reviewed physician journals are the most effective literature, such as:

- *Journal of the American Medical Association*

- *The New England Journal of Medicine*

- *Annals of Internal Medicine*

FIGURE 5.2 ◇ SAMPLE POA/PRESSURE ULCER QUERY

To Dr. _____

Date: _____

A skin "ulcer" or "wound" was documented in the medical record in addition to clinical indicators as CIRCLED below.

Chart location	Clinical Indicators	Comments
	Pictures on chart from wound care team	
	Other diagnoses: arteriosclerosis, diabetes, vascular disease, trauma, infection	
	Bed bound / Wheelchair bound	
	Wound care	
	Repositioning patient frequently	
	Egg crate mattress	
	Antibiotic ointment	
	Debridement	
	Other:	

Based on the criteria outlined above, can you please further SPECIFY the diagnosis, with the site(s), and the "POA" status?

Diagnosis:

	SKIN ULCER SPECIFIED?	SITE(S)	PRESENT on ADMISSION?
			Yes, No, Clinically Undetermined, Unknown
	Arteriosclerotic		
	Decubitus		
	Diabetic		
	Gangrenous		
	Varicose – Venous Stasis		
	Trauma – related, due to		
	Other		
	Unknown		

PHYSICIAN COMMENTS:

NOTE: The fact that a question is asked does not imply that any particular answer is desired or expected. Thank you.

Physician Signature: _____   Date _____

Source: James S. Kennedy.

Or specialty journals devoted to specific subspecialties, such as:

- *Stroke* for neurology

- *Critical Care Medicine* for critical care

- *Circulation* and the *Journal of the American College of Cardiology* for cardiology

Professional organizations often develop consensus or scientific statements that contain clinical definitions accepted by most physicians, such as:

- American Society of Infectious Disease

- American College of Cardiology

- American College of Chest Physicians

- National Kidney Foundation

- Society of Critical Care Medicine

- American Diabetes Association

Standard textbooks whose definitions are well accepted and used by most physicians can be employed as CDI references as well. Such texts include:

- *Textbook of Internal Medicine*

- *Textbook of Infectious Disease*

Coding Clinic *use in clinical determinations*

Although payer-based or coding resources, such as Medicare's national coverage determinations, the *Official Guidelines for Coding and Reporting*, and the American Hospital Association's *Coding Clinic for ICD-9-CM*, can be helpful if they support the previous mentioned resources, most physicians prefer to use the latest in medical literature when defining and diagnosing patient conditions. In fact, *Coding Clinic for ICD-9-CM*, First Quarter, 2008 opined that "the establishment of clinical parameters for code assignment is beyond the scope of authority of the Editorial Advisory Board for *Coding Clinic for ICD-9-CM*".[2]

Furthermore, the Third Quarter, 2008, edition stated:

> *Clinical information published in* Coding Clinic *does not constitute clinical criteria for establishing a diagnosis, substitute for the provider's clinical judgment, or eliminate the need for provider documentation regarding the clinical significance of a patient's medical condition.*[3]

Instead, *Coding Clinic for ICD-9-CM* supports the collaborative development of guidelines for querying physicians. It states:

> *Facilities can work together with their medical staff to develop facility-specific coding guidelines which promote the complete documentation needed for consistent coding assignment.*[4]

Increasingly, CDI programs have begun to maintain, and regularly update, a comprehensive set of clinical guidelines vetted by the medical staff most closely linked to the particular condition in question. For example, many facilities have clinical guidelines to help determine types of congestive heart failure based on recent medical literature and as supported by the cardiology department. Similarly, CDI programs have increasingly included coding and physician staff members in the development of query templates for the same reason.

Physician judgment

CDI program leaders should work with physicians to outline clinical indicators and definitions for "controversial" diagnoses. CDI programs must ensure that any such information is part of ongoing CDI and physician education and that it gets updated annually or at least as frequently as advances in regulations or healthcare standards demand. Although such efforts provide guidance to all parties, physicians can still determine a diagnosis based on his or her clinical judgment.

For example, when a patient presents with pneumonia, one of the clinical indicators would be an infiltrate on the chest x-ray. However, if the patient is severely dehydrated, the x-ray may not show an infiltrate. Similarly, if the patient is presenting with an acute exacerbation of congestive heart failure in addition to pneumonia, infiltrates may not be visible. In both of these examples, the physician can use their clinical judgment and assign a pneumonia diagnosis and treat accordingly.

Unfortunately, there are no exact answers when determining how much clinical evidence to include in a query. The key is finding the "sweet spot" wherein there is enough evidence to support a given diagnosis without overwhelming the reader.

Clinical evidence should generally include information from some or all of the following areas:

- Sign and symptoms with duration

- Diagnostic test results

- Lab findings

- Findings of consultants

- Treatment performed

For example, when writing a query for pneumonia the following information should be included:

- Signs and symptoms: fever 101°, green sputum, cough for a week

- Diagnostic test results: chest x-ray with left lower lobe infiltrate

- Lab findings: white blood cell count of 14,000

- Treatment: started on Levaquin intravenous (IV) piggyback (short-term infusion)

Notice this example did not include multiple sets of vital signs, as the diagnosis of pneumonia is primarily made based on signs and symptoms and radiological findings. Alternately, some diagnoses are less straightforward and require more clinical evidence to write a compliant query.

For example, when writing a query for a suspected case of acute renal failure, more in-depth information may be needed with the treatment and outcome tied together, such as:

- Signs and symptoms: Severe nausea and vomiting for one week and unable to keep down fluids. History of normal creatinine values prior to admission.

- Lab findings: Creatinine 3.6 at admission and decreased to 1.2 after 24 hours of IV fluid boluses.

- Findings of consultants: The nephrologist states "renal failure."

Those new to the CDI profession often struggle to determine the amount and type of clinical evidence to include with a query. *Coding Clinic for ICD-9-CM* goes on to say that such facility-specific policies can help provide instruction as to "when they should query physicians for clarification".[5]

Even though *Coding Clinic for ICD-9-CM* offers a variety of additional advice regarding when a clinical indicator (or lack thereof) may warrant the submission of a query (a comprehensive list of these instances is included in the appendix), the 2013 joint Association for Clinical Documentation Improvement Specialists (ACDIS)/AHIMA query practice brief "Guidelines for Achieving a Compliant Query Practice" warns that *Coding Clinic for ICD-9-CM* is neither an "authoritative" nor "comprehensive" resource for determining when queries may be appropriate.[6]

The 2013 ACDIS/AHIMA joint physician query brief states a query should be considered when the medical record "provides a diagnosis without underlying clinical validation." Furthermore, the 2013 query brief refers to Centers for Medicare & Medicaid Services (CMS) guidance published in its July 2011 Medicare *Quarterly Provider Compliance Newsletter*. In it, CMS instructs coders to:

> *refer to the* Coding Clinic *guidelines and query the physician when clinical validation is required. The practitioner does not have to use the criteria specifically outlined by* Coding Clinic, *but reasonable support within the health record for the diagnosis must be present.*[7]

Again, there is no magic formula for the amount of information to include in a query. AHIMA's 2008 guidance states:

> *Your [documentation] reviewer must use his or her professional judgment and discretion in considering the information contained on a hospital's physician query form along with the rest of the medical record.*[8]

CDI specialists need to use their clinical knowledge to think strategically and consider what the receiver of the information needs to make a clinical decision, without having to read a book report. In general, as long as the diagnosis and treatment is consistent throughout the documentation, a diagnosis should be assigned. Remember, by documenting a diagnosis, the physician is taking legal accountability for it. Nevertheless, if there is conflicting documentation and/or treatment, the attending physician should be queried to determine if the condition was ruled in or out.

Leading Queries

To lead or not to lead. The 2013 practice brief addressed the issue comparing the query role of CDI and coding staffs to an attorney questioning a witness in court. Just as an attorney cannot lead a witness, CDI specialists/coders cannot "lead healthcare providers with queries"[9].

Although not intended to limit conversations related to clinical care, the belief is that leading queries will compromise the integrity of coded data. The 2013 brief defines a leading query as "one that is not supported by the clinical elements in the health record and/or directs a provider to a specific diagnosis or procedure".[10] Additionally, it should not indicate the impact on reimbursement.

QUERY POINTS

The following are a few more pointers on submitting queries to a physician:

- Queries should be "guiding," not "leading"
- Queries should always include clinical evidence
- Never tell the physician what to write, no matter how clear the clinical picture appears
- Always phrase your query to the physician as a question
- Avoid having the query sound like a demand
- Avoid providing the expected answer in the question (implied leading)
- Avoid the words "you" and "but" in queries, as these words tend to trigger a defensive reaction and make others feel threatened
- Ask questions that can be responded to in a "yes" or "no" fashion
- Never indicate the financial impact of the response to the query
- Avoid queries that require only a physician signature

On the other hand, CDI specialists can encourage physicians to document:

- Their clinical concerns regarding a particular patient
- Interactions between disease processes
- Uncertain conditions
- Conditions being empirically treated
- The reason for patient retention
- The possible, probable, or suspected cause of symptoms
- Diagnoses resolved versus ruled out

Leading examples

In the following examples of inappropriate queries, the CDI specialist does not give the provider any documentation option other than the specific diagnosis requested. The statements are directive in nature, indicating what the provider should document rather than querying the provider for his or her professional determination of the clinical facts.

In the first example, the statement "the patient has anemia" may be presumptive, and the statement "please document 'acute blood loss anemia'" is directive and clearly leads the provider.

In the second example, the CDI specialist inappropriately asks the physician to document chronic respiratory failure. In the third example, the CDI specialist introduces new information not previously documented in the medical record. This is also inappropriate in a provider query. If this diagnosis was not documented in the current admission and is not affecting the patient's care, it does not meet the definition of a secondary diagnosis. Querying for this new information, which does not meet coding and reporting requirements, is inappropriate.

Concerns regarding leading queries are not new to the latest AHIMA query practice brief. Remember, recovery auditors can request queries as part of their medical record reviews, the Office of the Inspector General and Department of Justice have (and continue to) investigate claims of upcoding related to leading queries, and the 2008 AHIMA query practice brief states that "if the physician query form is leading in nature or if it introduces new information, the non-physician reviewer must refer the case to the physician reviewer."[11]

So, how does one ensure their query is not leading? The easiest way is to provide a clinical snapshot of the patient and ask an open-ended question. This type of query is appropriate in many cases but not all. Determining which type of query to use can be as important as identifying which clinical indicators to include within the query.

INAPPROPRIATE QUERIES

1. Dr. Smith—Based on your documentation, this patient has anemia and was transfused two units of blood. Also, there was a 10-point drop in hematocrit following surgery. Please document "acute blood loss anemia," as this patient clearly meets the clinical criteria for this diagnosis.

2. Dr. Jones—This patient has chronic obstructive pulmonary disease (COPD) and is on oxygen every night at home and has been on continuous oxygen since admission. Please document "chronic respiratory failure."

3. Dr. Phill—I reviewed the patient's last admission three weeks ago and saw a notation that the patient had candidiasis of mouth that was treated with Miracle mouthwash. Please clarify and document in the progress notes if the patient still has the condition.

APPROPRIATE QUERIES

1. Dr. Smith—In your progress note on 6/20, you documented anemia and ordered transfusion of two units of blood. Also, according to the lab work done on xx/xx, the patient had a 10-point drop in hematocrit following surgery. Based on these indications, please document, in the discharge summary, the type of anemia you were treating.

2. Dr. Jones—This patient has COPD and is on oxygen every night at home and has been on continuous oxygen since admission. Based on these indications, please indicate whether you were treating one of the following diagnoses:

   - Chronic respiratory failure
   - Acute respiratory failure
   - Acute on chronic respiratory failure
   - Hypoxia
   - Unable to determine
   - Other: _____

3. Dr. Phill—The H&P indicates the patient is complaining of mouth sores that started after his last inpatient chemo treatment. The orders indicate the patient is being treated with Miracle mouthwash. Please clarify the diagnosis being treated with Miracle Mouthwash.

Choosing the Right Format

Although the justification (clinical evidence) for a query must always be included, the query format may vary depending on the information missing, clinical situation, and the provider being queried.

Query formats include open ended, multiple choice, yes/no, verbal, etc. All these query format choices mean the person performing the query role must be able to think strategically to determine the best type of query for the clinical situation and physician involved.

Open-ended queries

The following is one example of a possible open-ended query: "Dear Dr. Phil, The patient's sodium (Na) was 129, the progress notes indicate low serum sodium level, '↓Na.' An order was written to place the patient on .9NS. Please clarify the associated diagnosis being treated." In this scenario, the physician is highly likely to respond and document "hyponatremia."

The 2013 ACDIS/AHIMA query practice brief describes an obtunded patient with a history of nausea and vomiting treated for pneumonia, as illustrated in Figure 5.3. The open-ended query asks the type/etiology of the pneumonia, which, in that example, most likely result in a response of "aspiration pneumonia".[12]

Sometimes an open-ended pneumonia query can be problematic, however. For example, "Dear Dr. Oz, the patient's progress note indicates he is being treated for pneumonia with vancomycin. Please clarify the type of pneumonia being treated."

Although the wording of this query does a great job of not leading, it may not result in the most clinically appropriate answer (methicillin-resistant *Staphylococcus aureus* pneumonia). In many cases, the physician will respond "bacterial pneumonia," which will still lack the specificity needed for coding purpose. Other physicians may respond "complex" or "severe" pneumonia.

In such situations, the CDI specialist would have to issue a second query in an attempt to further clarify the issue. The use of open-ended queries works best when the potential answers are limited, involve commonly used terminology, and when physicians essentially understand the type of documentation required.

FIGURE 5.3 ◇ **SAMPLE OPEN-ENDED QUERY**

A patient is admitted with pneumonia. The admitting H&P examination reveals WBC of 14,000; a respiratory rate of 24; a temperature of 102 degrees; heart rate of 120; hypotension; and altered mental status. The patient is administered an IV antibiotic and IV fluid resuscitation.

Leading: The patient has elevated WBCs, tachycardia, and is given an IV antibiotic for Pseudomonas cultured from the blood. Are you treating for sepsis?

Nonleading: Based on your clinical judgment, can you provide a diagnosis that represents the below-listed clinical indicators?

In this patient admitted with pneumonia, the admitting history and physical examination reveals the following:

- WBC 14,000
- Respiratory rate 24
- Temperature 102° F
- Heart rate 120
- Hypotension
- Altered mental status
- IV antibiotic administration
- IV fluid resuscitation

Please document the condition and the causative organism (if known) in the medical record.

Source: AHIMA "Guidance for Clinical Documentation Improvement Programs." *Journal of AHIMA* 81, no.5 (May 2010): expanded web version.

Yes/no queries

Based on the 2008 guidance "Managing an Effective Query Process," many in the CDI industry believed that yes/no queries were acceptable only with present-on-admission (POA) queries.[13]

At times, this left the CDI specialists in the awkward position of asking what seemed like a silly question or using really poor grammar.

For example, physicians frequently neglect to cross-document findings from the surgical pathology report. For most CDI specialists, the easiest way to deal with this situation would have been to query the physician and ask whether he or she agrees with the "path report." Concerned that such a yes/no question violated industry guidance, CDI specialists wrote open-ended queries, such as "Please clarify the clinical diagnosis associated with the stage 3 malignant ovarian cancer on the pathology report" or multiple-choice questions that included limited options or findings different from the pathology report, such as benign, pathology aberration, etc. In both cases, the phrasing tended to annoy physicians.

The 2013 AHIMA/ACDIS query brief expanded the compliant use of yes/no queries to include:

- Substantiating or further specifying a diagnosis already present (i.e., findings in pathology, radiology, and other diagnostic reports)

- Establishing a cause-and-effect relationship between documented conditions such as manifestation/etiology, complications, and conditions/diagnostic findings (i.e., hypertension and congestive heart failure, diabetes mellitus, and chronic kidney disease)

- Resolving conflicting documentation from multiple practitioners (i.e., asking the attending physician who is documenting "renal failure" if he agrees with the "CDK stage 4" documented by the renal consultant[14]

Based on the above-described guidelines, a yes/no format would never be appropriate for a new diagnosis. Moreover, to ensure a yes/no query is not leading, non-POA queries should include "other" and "clinically undetermined" options. The use of these additional options allows this format to meet the standard of not being leading, as it offers the physician numerous alternatives. Additional alternatives include "not clinically significant" and "integral to."

So, in the earlier example of a patient with a pathology report showing ovarian cancer, the following compliant yes/no query could be composed:

Dear Dr. OZ,
Please clarify and document in the progress notes; do you agree with the pathology report specifying "stage 3 malignant ovarian cancer?"

- Yes

- No

- Other

- Clinically undetermined

Additional examples of "yes/no" queries were illustrated in Figure 3.5 in Chapter 3.

Multiple-choice queries

The 2013 ACDIS/AHIMA query practice brief continues to support the use of multiple-choice queries and provides further guidance. It reinforces the importance of including "clinically significant and reasonable options" and including the clinical evidence.[15]

Many in the CDI industry were concerned about the use of multiple-choice queries when the reasonable choices were limited. For example, CDI specialists struggled on how to use a multiple-choice format when querying for a low serum sodium level. What diagnoses can they list in addition to hyponatremia? Hypernatremia would not be reasonable. Many were concerned that by listing only one diagnosis, they could be accused of leading the physician, even if "other" and "clinically undetermined" were used.

The 2013 ACDIS/AHIMA query practice brief recognizes that in some clinical situations, diagnoses may be limited. To resolve the concern, it suggests that queries should include additional options, such as "clinically undetermined" and "other" with space for the provider to add additional verbiage[16].

In some situations, such as the hyponatremia example given earlier, it may be appropriate to add options such as "not clinically significant." This would also be a good choice when querying about radiological and other test findings. Lastly, adding an option of "integral to" (and therefore should not be separately coded) may be appropriate. Some examples of when to consider the "integral to" option include:

- Clarifying the presence of a surgical complication. A nicked bowel that occurred while removing dense abdominal adhesions is generally not inherent; however, sometimes surgeons will state it is due to the location of the adhesions.

- Clarifying whether a diagnosis is an expected outcome (i.e., integral to) a surgery:

  - Ileus 48 hours post-laparoscopic appendectomy is not inherent, as it does not occur in most patients

– Ileus 24 hours post-colon resection is inherent, as it occurs in most patients

– Acute blood loss anemia after joint replacement procedures: answer tends to vary among surgeons

• Clarifying whether a diagnosis is integral to or inherent to the specific disease process:

– Cerebral edema is not inherent in cerebral hemorrhage, as it does not occur in most patients with this diagnosis

– Conversely, hypoxemia is inherent in acute respiratory failure, as it occurs in all patients with respiratory failure

Figure 5.4 illustrates an effective sample query to obtain additional specificity for the acuity of congestive heart failure as a secondary diagnosis.

FIGURE 5.4 ◇ SAMPLE MULTIPLE-CHOICE QUERY

A patient is admitted for a right hip fracture. The H&P notes that the patient has a history of chronic congestive heart failure. A recent echocardiogram showed left ventricular ejection fraction (EF) of 25 percent. The patient's home medications include metoprolol XL, lisinopril, and Lasix.

Leading: Please document if you agree the patient has chronic diastolic heart failure.

Nonleading: It is noted in the impression of the H&P that the patient has chronic congestive heart failure and a recent echocardiogram noted under the cardiac review of systems reveals an EF of 25 percent. Can the chronic heart failure be further specified as:

• Chronic systolic heart failure _____
• Chronic diastolic heart failure _____
• Chronic systolic and diastolic heart failure _____
• Some other type of heart failure _____
• Undetermined _____

Source: AHIMA. "Guidance for Clinical Documentation Improvement Programs." *Journal of AHIMA* 81, no.5 (May 2010): expanded web version.

Verbal queries

Historically, CDI specialists have been encouraged to perform their work on the patient floors in an effort to be visible to physicians and allow for verbal queries and documentation education moments.

Verbal queries have the advantage of engaging the physician for immediate feedback. Typical practice has been for the CDI staff to record the query and include a summary of the discussion. Unfortunately, time-stressed staff members sometimes cut corners and simply take credit for conducting the verbal query without recording the supporting information.

CDI specialist should document some notation of a verbal query for compliance purposes. The following information could be captured either on the patient concurrent review worksheet or in the CDI query electronic tracking tool:

POINTERS FOR CONDUCTING EFFECTIVE VERBAL QUERIES

The following lists provide a few "dos and don'ts" pointers for verbal queries.

Do:
- Demonstrate your knowledge of the topic
- Present the information concisely and clearly
- Plan your verbal interactions with physicians
- Be aware of your nonverbal communications
- Express appreciation of the physician's schedule
- Display an attitude of assistance
- Schedule meetings in advance to discuss CDI
- Allow time for physician feedback
- Provide guidance and education

Don't:
- Try to diagnose physicians' patients
- Approach physicians during a crisis/emergent situation
- Argue with the physician; reschedule the interaction instead
- Communicate the wrong message
- Display negative body language
- Continue a "negative" or "defensive" discussion with the physician

---

- Date of discussion

- Physician name

- Specific clarification/query topic

- Brief summary of discussion

- A paraphrase of the question with a paraphrase of the answer

This issue is addressed in the 2013 ACDIS/AHIMA query practice brief "Guidelines for Achieving a Compliant Query Practice," which states that:

- "Verbal queries should contain the same clinical indicators and follow the same format as written queries to ensure compliance and consistency in policy and process

- Documentation of the verbal query may be condensed to reflect the stated information but should identify the clinical indicators that support the query as well as the actual question posed to the practitioner

- Verbal queries should be documented at the time of the discussion or immediately following"[15]

One should never argue with the physician. They are responsible for the patient's care and know the patient's condition better than anyone. The goal of the CDI process is not to question the diagnosis itself but to have the patient's clinical condition documented with the most specific terminology in the medical record. It is sometimes better to let an issue go rather than risk offending a physician.

With electronic medical records, CDI specialists have the ability to work remotely. In these situations, fewer verbal queries are occurring, and those that do occur take place over the telephone. Although the means of communication may be different (phone versus face-to-face), the method is the same, and CDI specialists must be sure they record the query and the supporting clinical indicators for which it was needed.

VERBAL CLARIFICATION SCENARIOS

The following clinical scenarios illustrate where clarification would be indicated and examples of differing communication methods.

Clinical example: The record states the patient was admitted for treatment of pneumonia and the patient was placed on IV antibiotics. Sputum cultures obtained the day after admission showed growth of *Pseudomonas*. The physician subsequently ordered a change in antibiotics as recommended by the sensitivity report. For the coder to assign a code for *Pseudomonas* pneumonia, this relationship between the pneumonia and the organism needs to be documented in the record.

Approach #1 (verbal query): "Dr. Phil, I'm Jane from the Documentation Improvement team. Do you have a minute to clarify something? I noted that the patient's C/S showed growth of *Pseudomonas* and that you changed the antibiotics when the sputum culture results were available. Do you feel that the *Pseudomonas* may have been the causative organism? You do? Could you please clarify that cause-and-effect relationship in the record? You could document the relationship as either '*Pseudomonas* pneumonia' or 'pneumonia due to *Pseudomonas*.' Thanks for your help."

Approach #2 (verbal query): "Dr. Phil, I'm Jane from the Documentation Improvement team. Do you have a minute to clarify something? Not now? Thanks, I appreciate that you're busy. I'll leave a written request in the record and you can provide your answer in [the progress notes, history and physical, electronic medical records inbox, etc.] when you make rounds tomorrow. Thanks so much for your time. If I have any additional questions, I'll let you know."

The second method requires additional follow-up by the CDI specialist to ensure that the clarification was provided; however, it's better than insisting that the physician do it immediately and risk angering (or alienating) that provider.

Clinical example: A feeble, deconditioned 83-year-old patient was admitted for treatment of a fractured hip caused by a fall. An open reduction, internal fixation was performed the day after admission. The patient has had several previous admissions over the past 12 months for other conditions. The patient's BUN and creatinine levels were elevated on admission, and a review of the patient's previous renal studies showed that the admitting serum creatinine was >50% than baseline for this patient. IV fluid boluses followed by IV fluids at an eight-hour rate were initiated with orders to repeat the renal panel daily. The patient's serum creatinine has been steadily improving since the preceding interventions were implemented. The record states "increased creatinine/renal insufficiency."

Approach #1 (verbal query): "Dr. Jones, I'm Joe from the Documentation Improvement team. Do you have a minute to clarify something? Great, thanks. I noted that the patient's creatinine was increased more than 50% over his baseline on admission and that the progress notes said 'renal insufficiency.' The history and physical also alluded to his slowly worsening renal function. Do these findings meet your definition of 'acute on chronic renal failure'? They do? Would you please clarify that in your next note? Thanks for your assistance."

Approach #2 (verbal query): "Dr. Jones, I'm Joe from the Documentation Improvement team. Do you have a minute to clarify something? Great, thanks. I noted that the patient's creatinine was increased more than 50% over his baseline on admission and that the progress notes said 'renal insufficiency' and 'hypertension.' The history and physical also alluded to his slowly worsening renal function. Do these findings meet your definition of 'acute on chronic renal failure'? They don't? Would you say that the labs represent progression of his underlying chronic kidney disease (CKD)? You would? Would you please clarify the stage of the CKD and whether the kidney disease is related to his hypertension? Thanks for your assistance."

In the preceding scenario, the physician disagreed with the first question but was willing to document the condition posed in the second question. The physician does not have to agree with your request. He or she may disagree because he or she knows the patient's history better than what is captured in the current or previous records. Or he or she may disagree with your definition of "acute renal failure." The goal is to obtain greater specificity and accuracy, not always the highest-severity condition.

The next couple of years will be an exciting time of change for the healthcare industry. This concept was reinforced in the 2013 ACDIS/AHIMA query practice brief which states:

> *As healthcare delivery continues to evolve, it is expected that future revisions will be required.*[16]

As part of this change, those conducting physician queries have a powerful role in ensuring data and reimbursement accuracy and program compliance. The following quote from the 2013 ACDIS/AHIMA query practice brief best summarizes the goal of a CDI query:

> *A proper query process ensures that appropriate documentation appears in the health record. Personnel performing the query function should focus on a compliant query process and content reflective of appropriate clinical indicators to support the query. When CDI leadership take this goal to heart and follow both the letter and the spirit of the law, compliance will follow.*[17]

REFERENCES

1. Centers for Disease Control. *Official Guidelines for Coding and Reporting. www.cdc.gov/nchs/data/icd9/icdguide10.pdf.*

2. American Hospital Association (AHA). *Coding Clinic for ICD-9-CM, First Quarter, 2008*, p. 3.

3. AHA. *Coding Clinic for ICD-9-CM, Third Quarter, 2008*, p. 15.

4. AHA. *Coding Clinic for ICD-9-CM, First Quarter, 2000, p. 12.*

5. Ibid.

6. American Health Information Association (AHIMA). "Guidelines for Achieving a Compliant Query Practice*." Journal of AHIMA,* Vol. 84, No. 2, February 2013. *http://library.ahima.org/xpedio/groups/public/documents/ahima/bok1_050018.hcsp?dDocName= bok1_050018.*

7. Centers for Medicare and Medicaid Services (CMS). "Medicare Quarterly Provider Compliance Newsletter." Volume 1, Issue 4. July 2011.

8. AHIMA. "Managing an Effective Query Process." *Journal of AHIMA,* Vol. 79, No. 10, October 2008. *http://library.ahima.org/xpedio /groups/public/documents/ahima/bok1_040394.hcsp?dDocName=bok1_040394.*

9. AHIMA. "Guidelines for Achieving a Compliant Query Practice*." Journal of AHIMA,* Vol. 84, No. 2, February 2013. *http://library. ahima.org/xpedio/groups/public/documents/ahima/bok1_050018.hcsp?dDocName=bok1_050018.*

10. Ibid.

11. AHIMA. "Managing an Effective Query Process." *Journal of AHIMA,* Vol. 79, No. 10, October 2008. *http://library.ahima.org/xpedio /groups/public/documents/ahima/bok1_040394.hcsp?dDocName=bok1_040394.*

12. AHIMA. "Guidelines for Achieving a Compliant Query Practice*." Journal of AHIMA,* Vol. 84, No. 2, February 2013. *http://library .ahima.org/xpedio/groups/public/documents/ahima/bok1_050018.hcsp?dDocName=bok1_050018.*

13. AHIMA. "Managing an Effective Query Process." *Journal of AHIMA,* Vol. 79, No. 10, October 2008. *http://library.ahima.org/xpedio /groups/public/documents/ahima/bok1_040394.hcsp?dDocName=bok1_040394.*

14. AHIMA. "Guidelines for Achieving a Compliant Query Practice*." Journal of AHIMA,* Vol. 84, No. 2, February 2013.

15. Ibid.

16. Ibid.

17. Ibid.

Query and Documentation Improvement Outcomes

Clinical documentation improvement (CDI) specialists often seek definitions for realistic productivity benchmarks. Unfortunately, productivity standards depend on how a given facility establishes the responsibilities and expectations of its team. Therefore, before assessing CDI program success, goals defining that success need to be set.

Frequently, CDI efforts begin with review of Medicare records, because these typically represent the largest payer of hospital inpatient stays. Similarly, programs target financial incentives first, asking for clarification for documentation related to complications and comorbid (CC) conditions or major complications and comorbid (MCC) diagnoses to improve Medicare severity diagnosis-related group (MS-DRG) assignment, thereby increasing the relative weight (RW) and reimbursement for the care provided.

With the implementation of MS-DRGs, the Centers for Medicare & Medicaid Services (CMS) expected facilities to take advantage of opportunities for improved documentation.[1]

As programs begin their review efforts, most target "low-hanging fruit," typically underdocumented and underreported medical conditions. By monitoring CDI staff members' effectiveness on these targets, program managers can then make the case for additional staff and program expansion to other areas. Common targets include the following MS-DRG pairs and/or triplets and/or specific MS-DRGs with MCC/CC:

- Complex versus simple pneumonia (MS-DRG 177–179/MS-DRG 193–195)

- Sepsis versus urosepsis (MS-DRG 871–872/MS-DRG 689–690)

- Acute respiratory failure versus chronic obstructive pulmonary disease or congestive heart failure (MS-DRG 189/MS-DRG 190–192/MS-DRG 291–293)

- Stroke versus transient ischemic attack (MS-DRG 064–066/MS-DRG 069)

- Heart failure (MS-DRG 291–293)

- Gastrointestinal bleed (MS-DRG 377–379)

Additional information about tracking and monitoring MS-DRGs and the case mix index to quantify CDI program success are discussed later in this chapter. Of course, the preceding list is not all-inclusive, and CDI staff members need to understand that these areas represent targets for the Office of the Inspector General and Recovery Auditors, too. These organizations will look for spikes in facility reporting for a given diagnosis over another. Auditors will then review the records to ensure such conditions were actually present, documented, and treated and not simply documented once and "upcoded."

Although CDI efforts may start with a single payer and target high-risk areas, ideally all records and all payers for all conditions will fall under CDI purview. Setting program goals, and thereby productivity standards, depends on the experience of the staff and the capabilities of the facility.

Productivity

The productivity of CDI specialists who focus only on the CC/MCC capture will be very different from those asked to review records for quality indicators, present-on-admission (POA) conditions, admission status, and/or core measures. A record with seven days' worth of information requires more time to review than a two-day stay. It takes less time to review a paper record versus an electronic record. A blended record (part paper, part electronic) takes more time to review than an all-paper or all-electronic record. The more items requiring analysis and query efforts, the fewer number of charts can be reviewed in a given day.

Furthermore, CDI programs that aim to review all records regardless of payer will have additional record volume and will need additional staff or more focused efforts. Productivity standards also need to incorporate all the ancillary responsibilities of CDI programs. Query submission may well be the primary tool CDI specialists employ, but the time needed to work with coders and (HIM) professionals, develop physician education materials, attend CDI education sessions, and communicate with connected departments such as case management and quality, all need to be factors in the equation.

Staff experience

Assignments and years of CDI experience also determine productivity levels. For example, if a CDI staff member with little cardiac experience is assigned to review the telemetry floors or the cardiovascular intensive care unit, those reviews may take longer. Similarly, a seasoned veteran should be able to perform a thorough review on more charts than a new reviewer.

A brand new CDI specialist who just completed classroom training should be able to review six to 10 charts per day—a combination of new admissions and secondary reviews. New staff, trained "on the job," without formal classroom education, will take longer to get up to speed because their core knowledge depends on their colleagues' abilities to teach and mentor them. An initial chart review will take the novice CDI specialist approximately 30 to 45 minutes. This time remains fairly consistent until he or she internalizes the review process, memorizes common opportunities, and becomes more confident formatting physician queries.

When hiring a new CDI specialist, consider communication skills as one of the top qualities required for the job. The American Health Information Management Association (AHIMA) recommends CDI professionals maintain competencies in the following areas:

- Knowledge of healthcare regulations, including reimbursement and documentation requirements

- Clinical knowledge with training in pathophysiology

- Ability to read and analyze all information in a patient's health record

- Established channels of communication with providers and other clinicians

- Demonstrated skills in clinical terminology, coding, and classification systems

- Ability to apply coding conventions, official guidelines, and *Coding Clinic* advice to health record documentation[2]

In general, a dedicated, experienced CDI specialist should have an average daily census of 12 to 15 new patients and between five and 10 established/follow-up cases. Figure 6.1 illustrates an example of the volume of chart reviews for one CDI specialist in one week. On Monday there are 10 new admissions, so a total of 10 reviews are needed. On Tuesday there are nine new admissions plus 10 re-reviews

FIGURE 6.1 ◇ CHART REVIEWS PER DAY

	Monday	Tuesday	Wednesday	Thursday	Friday
	10	9	8	7	6
		10	9	8	7
			10	9	8
				10	9
					10
Total	**10**	**19**	**27**	**34**	**40**

Number of Chart Reviews and Re-reviews

Source: Lynne Spryszak, RN, CPC-A, CCDS.

from Monday's census, for a total of 19 reviews. By Friday, when you add the needed re-reviews to new admissions, the CDI specialist has a total of 40 charts to review for that day. This is a reasonable assignment for seasoned reviewers, as the assumption is that re-reviews do not require as much time as new admissions. (Review additional information on regarding benchmarks in the materials download section of this book.)

Bear in mind that the CDI staff members generally work Monday to Friday, so their actual daily census will be especially high on Mondays. However, many facilities are moving to a more flexible schedule to include a rotating day of the weekend and different staggered shifts in order to be available to the medical staff. Program managers generally determine schedules based on what works for each facility.

Also, when determining coverage, it's necessary to take into account various patient lengths of stay to make sure one CDI specialist does not have the majority of his or her census turning over on a daily basis.

Lastly, determine whether the CDI staff will be floor based (assigned to a nursing floor or unit) or physician based (assigned to a particular physician and his or her patients regardless of the patient's location within the hospital). Each option has advantages and disadvantages to consider. For example, being floor based may increase productivity; however, it may diminish the relationship between the physician and CDI specialist. One good practice is to routinely (on a quarterly basis) rotate staff members through all hospital units or specialties so every member of the team can confidently identify opportunities no matter what the clinical area.

Staffing ratios

An average rule of thumb is for a CDI program to employ one CDI specialist for every 1,200 to 1,500 discharges per year. A higher staff ratio should be considered for programs that expect their CDI specialist to perform multiple functions (core measures, etc.) and a lower ratio for programs that perform condition clarification only. As program expectations change, the staffing requirements should be reviewed again to ensure that the program's new goals are attainable with the resources available.[3]

Therefore, the decision of how many new staff members to hire can be made by dividing the average daily census by 15. CDI leaders can further quantify that number by obtaining the average daily admission numbers.

Query timing

The decision of when to query the physician represents an important aspect of the CDI program. In a perfect world, all cases would be reviewed within the first 24 hours of admission. However, due to staffing considerations, this may not always be possible. Some argue reviews performed too early result in unnecessary queries because the physician may not yet have enough information to determine the possible underlying diagnosis. Conversely, others support early reviews—including reviews in the emergency department—to ensure documentation of the underlying cause of admission and any present-on-admission indicators and to help physicians capture appropriate documentation for their evaluation and management records.[4]

At a minimum, reviews within the first 24 hours make the most sense. As the program matures (and the physicians' education levels increase), the CDI staff members may find expanding to the emergency department makes sense or that reviewing the chart at the 48-hour mark is more efficient.

Reviews should be conducted based on a few priorities, including:

- Patients with a symptom diagnosis

- Patients with high-risk DRGs (pneumonia, sepsis, transient ischemic attack, etc.)

- Patients in DRGs with a relative weight (RW) of less than 0.6

Additionally, CDI staff should prioritize any open queries and follow-up with physicians who did not respond to previous requests.

Those records, which revealed no initial query opportunities, should be reassessed on a 48- to 72-hour basis, especially as the patient becomes more stable and nears discharge. At this point, the CDI specialist should look for cases in which:

- Only symptom diagnoses are documented

- A CC/MCC is missing despite the patient's extended length of stay

- A length of stay greater than three days without documentation of associated severity or risk of mortality

- The patient discharge was expected but canceled

- A stage 2 to stage 4 decubitus ulcer is documented, to capture potential documentation for excisional debridement

Query ratios

Most new programs have a query percentage benchmark of 30% to 40%. Basically, this means that every 100 reviews should yield query opportunities 30% of the time. This is a broad guideline—sometimes five reviews yield no opportunities for clarification, and sometimes five reviews yield five opportunities. This performance measure shouldn't be applied to individual reviewers but to the program overall because more opportunities exist on medical or surgical units, for example, than on pediatric or obstetric units.

This measurement should shift over time as well. Theoretically, physicians will learn to document acute on chronic systolic heart failure and the type of pneumonia, thereby decreasing the need for queries.

To draft reasonable expectations for the percent of queries expected, conduct annual audits aimed at uncovering additional documentation opportunities and chart the percentage of those records that contain those opportunities. For example, out of 100 records, an additional severity of illness measure could have been captured in 35 of them. Reset your CDI query expectations for these measures, educate CDI staff and physicians of the reason for the expansion, and then readjust the query expectation rate for the program and that particular measure.

Determining the query rate by reviewer per day varies also by experience, query type, etc. Programs without sufficient physician education can expect a higher number of queries generated per day than if the physicians had foreknowledge about the program's goals at the outset. If physicians have no idea what is expected of them and no information about how their documentation affects quality and reporting, the only way to obtain improved documentation is on a case-by-case basis, which is inefficient and time-consuming for both the CDI team and the physician.

Even with preparatory education, a new program should expect that, initially, there will be larger volumes of queries for specific conditions (e.g., acute on chronic systolic heart failure) and a corresponding increased volume of queries for comorbidities associated with specific diagnoses that heretofore were omitted: cerebral edema with cerebral hemorrhage, for example, or septic shock with sepsis instead of "hypotension."

It is a false assumption that a program should be generating the same volume of queries every month, and even over time, if the program makes sufficient effort to provide physicians with ongoing information. Using the percentage of queries written as a benchmark really measures how well the team fails to change physician documentation patterns. It's like saying, "We had a 60% query rate last month—we are so good at failing!" And yet, hospital executives, who do not understand the data, may interpret low query rates as evidence of poor performance and/or productivity. Neither should queries disappear altogether. As codes changes, CC/MCC designations shift, and payment/quality reporting requirements advance, CDI specialists will need to monitor documentation needs, educate physicians, and query staff as needed.

A better way to measure performance is to use query:

- Volume (rate of queries compared to number of records reviewed)

- Response (rate of queries answered by physicians)

- Agreement (number of queries physicians agreed with which resulted in additional documentation)

- Type (percentage of verbal, multiple-choice, open-ended, yes/no questions submitted)[5]

These data should be captured and analyzed by individual CDI specialist, by physician, and by the overall program results. Such analysis may well show an educational opportunity for CDI staff on malnutrition documentation and coding. It may show that one CDI staff member primarily asks verbal queries and may need assistance composing written ones. It may show that every time a particular physician receives a query about kidney disease, he or she ignores it. The data allow CDI staff to uncover underlying trouble spots and target education for improvement. (For additional audit information, read the white paper "Audit Your Program to Avoid Pitfalls" in the materials download section of this book.)

Month-to-month variability in data will exist, but it is important to be aware of how the data accrue and are used so that they can be interpreted in relationship to staffing changes (vacation, etc.), physician information (increases or decreases in physician compliance), or coding/CDI communication (improvement or breakdown of coding/CDI specialist interactions). Examination of these elements over time, quarter over quarter, year over year, can illustrate the CDI team's progress and highlight individual reviewer efforts against team successes.

Query Effectiveness

"Documentation can be greatly improved by a properly functioning query process," AHIMA says in its 2008 "Managing an Effective Query Process" practice brief. Facilities need to determine how that process works before they can analyze whether it works successfully or not. The first step is to establish policies and procedures for how and when to query. These policies should be clearly communicated to the CDI staff and reviewed annually to appropriately reflect changes in industry guidance. Because query policies and procedures define standards for the query process, they serve as a generally accepted common ground for when it comes time to audit queries for effectiveness.[6]

Creating query policies

At a minimum, CDI programs should develop policies and procedures dictating expectations for its staff. These should incorporate the latest query guidance information as well as relevant citations regarding the importance of query responses. (The appendix of this book includes a sample policy for adaptation. Additional policies are available in the Association of Clinical Documentation Improvement Specialists [ACDIS] Forms & Tools Library.)

Internal policies define the query process and each professional's role. Make sure policies and procedures are vetted and can hold up to scrutiny. Then make sure everyone in the CDI and health information management (HIM) departments receives training on the process and consistently adheres to it.

Query retention

The issue of whether to retain written queries as a permanent part of the medical record (or whether to retain them at all) has been a matter of some controversy among compliance officers and hospital attorneys. The 2013 ACDIS/AHIMA physician query practice brief encourages facilities to craft policies around this matter, as discussed in Chapter 4.[7]

Some believe making queries part of the medical record creates an unnecessary liability and can open the facility to recovery auditor vulnerabilities. Others believe CDI query forms/programs should be transparent and used to defend against recovery auditor and OIG scrutiny.[8]

If the queries are not part of the permanent medical record, define how the forms will be retained and where and how they will be accessed when needed. The 2008 AHIMA query practice brief "Managing an Effective Query Practice" calls on facilities to address the permanence and retention of the completed query form. It recommends programs refer to applicable state guidelines to ensure compliance.[9]

Physician response

Determining parameters for physicians' responses to queries should incorporate the convenience of the physician as well as the needs of the coding and CDI staff. For example, facilities which determine that query forms will be retained as a permanent part of the medical record may permit the physician to respond to the query directly on the form as long as sufficient documentation also exists in the body of the medical record.

Each facility should check with its state Quality Improvement Organization (QIO) for guidelines. Additional options include:

- We will accept the query as a progress note, as long as the document was signed, dated, timed, and created in the normal course of the chart (i.e., concurrently, at time of coding, or within the medical staff general rules and regulations within 30 days of discharge).

- We accept the response to the query on the actual query form, unless the query posed a leading question or introduced information not documented in the medical record. We follow the basic standards outlined in the AHIMA physician query practice brief.

- We do not accept coding summary forms (e.g., physician query forms) as documentation in the medical record when following diagnosis-related group (DRG) validation procedures. There should be an addendum in the medical record that is signed and dated by the physician.

If the program employs a physician advisor, set parameters for his or her involvement in the program to determine the level of involvement and his or her participation in closing outstanding queries. The physician advisor has the ability to speak peer-to-peer and ideally is perceived as an authority figure by other physicians. This influence can often mean the difference between physician acceptance and participation with CDI goals or complete rejection of the program.

If the facility has done a good job educating the stakeholders, the number of "no responses" to queries should be minimal. It is unreasonable to expect a 100% query response rate. A more realistic goal would perhaps be 90% to 95%.[10]

All methods of finalizing queries should be considered: calls to the physician by the CDI specialist and/or physician advisor, developing an easier way for physicians to comply (fax query forms, electronic query forms, etc.), as well as strong support from administration to support the program's processes.

Facilities increasingly consider lack of response to physician queries a "medical record deficiency." As such, many programs include escalation policies and some even escalate lack of response as a detriment to a physician's credentialing privileges. In some respects, such actions represent a more immediate consequence for those physicians hesitant to support the program. It acts as the proverbial stick to the carrot of improved documentation for quality of care considerations.

Regardless of the punishment related to the physician's lack of response to a query, the CDI team and administrators must include some language in its policies and procedures governing what CDI staff should do when a particular physician does not respond. Many include expectations, such as:

> *CDI associate will follow up on an unanswered query within the first 24 hours. A provider has 48 hours to answer a concurrent query. If the query is not answered, the query will be escalated to the CDI program manager and/or designee. The specific site physician advisor is then consulted as needed.*

The following sample policy regarding query escalation and resolution addresses the specific timing expectations for query responses.

The sample policy also addresses how CDI staff should communicate with coders and physician advisors and under what circumstances. Further, as recently encouraged by the 2013 ACDIS/AHIMA query brief, it addresses what circumstances might warrant raising an unanswered query to the attention of a CDI or HIM manager, physician advisor, or higher level administrator. Figure 6.2 illustrates the hierarchy of possible query escalation.

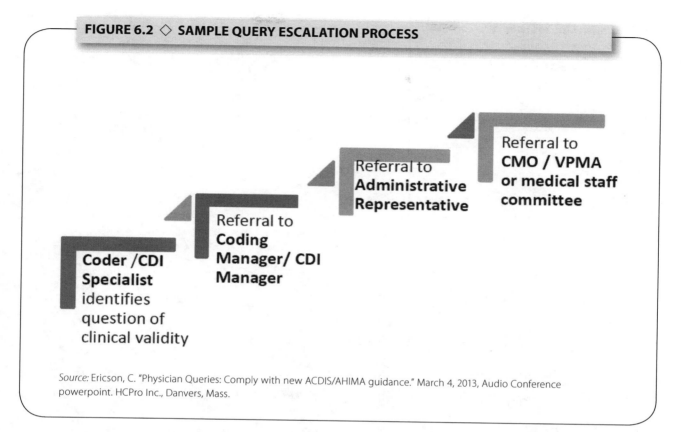

FIGURE 6.2 ◇ SAMPLE QUERY ESCALATION PROCESS

Source: Ericson, C. "Physician Queries: Comply with new ACDIS/AHIMA guidance." March 4, 2013, Audio Conference powerpoint. HCPro Inc., Danvers, Mass.

SAMPLE ESCALATION AND RESOLUTION POLICY

Query Review Process
Policy Manual:
Effective Date:
Revised Date:

Policy 1: Unanswered Queries

If the query is unanswered at the time of discharge, the CDI specialist is to come to HIM and review the record to see if the physician has answered the question.

If a review of the record indicates that the question has been answered, the chart will proceed to be coded.

If, at the time of coding there the chart still needs clarification, the coder will generate a retrospective query form and contact the CDI specialist reviewer nurse to pursue further follow-up with the physician.

The review nurse will contact the physician's office by phone to notify them and request a prompt reply.

If the fax query is returned within 48 hours to the designated coder, the coder will return the query to the principal coder for completion.

A designated coder will notify the review nurse via e-mail that a response was obtained. If the nurse is not notified within 48 hours that a reply was received, she can assume that no response was obtained.

Advisor for follow-up who will contact the physician in question.

The physician will then have 72 hours (business days) to respond. If no response is obtained after 72 hours and a query response would result in greater than $500 (RW change of .10) in revenue, the case will then be referred to the VP of Medical Affairs for further action.

If a response is still not obtained after 36 hours (business days) and the reimbursement potential is greater than or equal to $10,000, the case will then be escalated to the chief executive officer or chief financial officer for further action, as determined.

Policy 2: General Communication

If there is a discrepancy between the CDI specialist and coder interpretation of the medical record, resulting in the assignment of a lower-weighted DRG (i.e., change in principal diagnosis, omission of a MCC/CC, alternate procedure), a discussion will take place between the coder and the CDI specialist, at a time arranged via phone, e-mail, or page.

If, after discussion, consensus is still not reached, the chart will be referred to the CDI Physician Advisor for review and the coding manager will be notified by the coder of such cases (so as to account for all uncoded charts).

If, during or after coding a record, the coder identifies the need to query the physician, the coder will contact one of the CDI specialists to initiate the above "unanswered query process" to obtain further clarification.

If the need for a MCC/CC or capture of the appropriate SOI/ROM remains after the DRG analyst has analyzed the chart, and querying the physician might result in increased reimbursement or SOI/ROM, the CDI specialist will be contacted to initiate the "unanswered query process" above to obtain further clarification.

The coding summary sheet, which is to be attached to all CDI worksheets, will be notated by the coder in the lower corner or the summary sheet as follows:

"CDI Specialist" if a CDI Specialist worksheet was generated for that record

"PA" if the CDI Physician Advisor reviewed the record

"DRG" if the record went to the DRG analyst for additional review

Policy 3: General Guidelines for consulting the Physician Advisor

- if consensus is not reached between the coder and the nurse and such analysis would result in additional reimbursement of ≥ $500.00 or greater SOI/ROM.
- when an immediate clinical decision is needed after the CDI Specialist are gone for the day, or on the weekend. In these cases, the CDI Specialist will be notified of such action via e-mail or voice mail.
- All cases reviewed by the CDI Physician Advisor will be noted (as above) on the coding summary worksheet or, if no summary sheet is attached, on the CDI worksheet, so that a record may be kept for tracking and quality purposes.

Source: Spryszak, L. ACDIS. Forms & Tools Library. "Unanswered query and query conflict escalation policy."

Multiple-query policies

Previous controversy regarding whether the AHIMA query practice brief guidance could (or should) be applied to CDI efforts overall led to the argument for, and creation of, separate query policies for coder- and nursing-based CDI professionals. Specifically, many argued that one policy, permitting casual conversations regarding clinical indicators, was permissible for the clinical CDI specialist engaged in concurrent documentation clarification and a second policy for a coder performing targeted, coding-related retrospective queries.

For example, proponents believe clinicians could concurrently leave a query that states:

> *The patient has a GI bleed, documentation of anemia (Hbg 8.2), and treatment with one unit of packed red blood cells. Is this acute blood loss anemia?*

Opponents of the two-guideline philosophy believe a query written this way is leading and should be open ended, as in "please indicate the type of anemia," or should include multiple choices with "other" and "unable to clinically determine" options.

Because it was a joint publication, the most recent ACDIS/AHIMA 2013 "Guidelines for Achieving a Compliant Query Practice" cemented the applicability of the guidance to both CDI and coding/HIM staff members and essentially eliminated the debate.[11]

Furthermore, the American Hospital Association (AHA) *Coding Clinic for ICD-9-CM, First Quarter, 2000,* supports the development of uniform guidelines for querying physicians. It states:

> *Any guidelines developed must be applied consistently to all records coded. These facility guidelines must not conflict with the* Official ICD-9-CM Guidelines for Coding and Reporting.[12]

Those who had different rules depending on staff performing the query or timing of the query (retrospective versus concurrent) should review and revise those policies to conform to the latest guidance. Government agencies will not care who asked the question or when, if the query leads the physician to document in an inappropriate way. No matter who asks the question or when they ask it, the query needs to generate an honest clinical opinion of the diagnosis or procedure performed. The content of any question should include the clinical indicators, and the answer/documentation should be consistently used.

Retrospective efforts

CDI program and facility administrators need to make several decisions related to the retrospective query process and chart reconciliation. They must collaboratively choose which department owns the retrospective query process or decide whether the process of performing the retrospective query should be divided up based on particular circumstances. For example, the CDI staff may be responsible for obtaining a query answer retrospectively when the physician did not answer the query they issued prior to discharge.

Alternatively, HIM may be responsible for obtaining answers related to POA issues or cases not reviewed concurrently by the CDI staff. Other determinations include:

- The role of HIM in conducting retrospective queries related to clinical information introduced after the chart was last reviewed by the CDI specialist

- Which department will work with physicians to obtain missing documentation from discharge summaries that was present in the progress notes during the course of the stay

- How long to hold a patient's chart when awaiting the physician's response to a query, if the query will impact DRG assignment

- How long to hold a patient's chart when awaiting a physician's response to a severity of illness query that does not influence the DRG assignment

Figure 6.3 illustrates typical retrospective query issues and their common solutions and the pros and cons for each.

Retrospective queries should be done as soon as possible postdischarge prior to billing, but definitely within seven days of discharge, so that the query may be answered and the medical record completed within the 14- to 30-day deadlines established by states, the CMS, and The Joint Commission. Although there are no official timelines for correcting a record, the moment a notice from an attorney, Recovery Auditor, or OIG official is received is definitely not the time to add an addendum, clarification, or late entry.

FIGURE 6.3 ◇ RETROSPECTIVE QUERY SOLUTIONS

Common query reconciliation issues	Responsible party	Pros	Cons
Concurrent query not answered that affects the DRG Discharge summary nullifies a concurrent query (dissonance in the medical record) Concurrent query results in a diagnosis without a clear indication of whether it was POA	HIM	Allows CDI staff to focus on new cases. Better response rate from physicians if they are accustomed to HIM asking queries after discharge.	May take longer to obtain an answer, which will negatively affect DNFB (discharged not final billed). The CDS staff may not be as diligent in obtaining an answer concurrently as others will take care of it on the back end.
	CDI	Generally allows for a quicker answer, which lessens the impact on DNFB (discharged not final billed). When performed immediately, will promote more accurate physician responses. Ensures that CDS staff members own their queries and work to improve their processes.	May take time away from concurrent charts. Physicians may be annoyed at being asked to clarify a discharged case. If chart is taken to the floor by CDS, will need to ensure that regulations pertaining to the Health Insurance Portability and Accountability Act of 1996 are followed. May be disagreement between HIM and CDS as to what is a CDI type of query and what is a coding issue type of query.

Source: James S. Kennedy.

CDI/coder agreement

Many programs track the agreement rates between coders and CDI specialists on their monthly dashboards or reports. Also known as "reconciliation," this process is where the diagnoses are finalized prior to final billing and any differences between CDI specialists and HIM/coding staff determinations are discussed. Many facilities have a policy defining the steps taken by the CDI specialist and coder to discuss a mismatch record prior to final billing, and many have found that emphasizing adherence to these policies prevents conflict and program breakdown over time. (A sample policy is included in the downloads section of this book.)

Tracking DRG mismatches is another example of a metric that has some merit for beginning programs but loses importance as time goes on. Initially, novice CDI teams will have a low ratio of agreement as each department learns the new processes and gains comfort and expertise. By the end of the first year, the CDI specialist and coder should have the same diagnoses/DRGs at least 65% to 75% of the time. Mature programs will show even higher concordance due to their experience levels and due to the establishment of, and adherence to, effective communication policies.

Nevertheless, agreement rates should be monitored on a consistent basis as large variability in the ratio may indicate a need for intervention. If the number of records final-billed without a CC or MCC begins to rise, further investigation may be warranted to ascertain the reason.

Decreases in concurrence might include staffing shortages. If the CDI staff has to review more records, he or she will have less time for secondary reviews and query follow-ups. If there is a coder staff member shortage, he or she may not have time to respond to CDI specialists' questions or feel pressure to simply code the case and pass it over to billing. A change in staffing expertise, new personnel unaware of the reconciliation processes, and other factors also affect the agreement rate between coders and CDI staff. Whatever the reasons, monitoring on a regular basis can help programs identify and resolve discrepancies early.

One of the biggest mistakes CDI program leadership can do is to ignore or react punitively when the CDI specialists' final DRG does not match the coded DRG. These situations, commonly known as DRG mismatches, may occur for a variety of reasons, including the:

- CDI specialist did not assign the correct DRG

- Documentation changed after the record was last reviewed by the CDI specialist

- Discharge summary contraindicated previous documentation

- Coder did not assign the correct DRG based on physician documentation

- CDI specialist and the coder misinterpreted the clinical circumstances

Regardless of the reason, the reconciliation of these DRG mismatches represents a learning opportunity for all involved if proactively addressed. A robust conversation of the discrepancies can lead a CDI specialist to deeper understanding of the coding rules and regulations and help coders better understand the clinical thinking of the CDI staff. Used as a learning tool, discussion of DRG mismatches also represents a good way to foster mutual respect and understanding of the various teams' knowledge base and job responsibilities.

An effective CDI program should include a method of tracking the final DRG assigned by the CDI specialist and the final DRG assigned by the coding staff on a case-by-case basis. The CDI specialist that performed the last review of the case should be responsible for reconciling the case with the coder. This process can occur on a daily to weekly basis and involves the CDI specialist examining the notes of the case against the codes assigned by HIM.

By reviewing these codes and comparing them to their notes on the case, they can generally determine why the DRG did not match. Common reasons include the:

- Patient had a surgical procedure after they were last reviewed by the CDI specialist

- Coder found a CC or MCC missed by the CDI specialist

- Physician nullified or added a new diagnosis in the discharge summary

- CDI specialist assigned a different diagnosis as the principal

Sometimes, the CDI specialist may not be able to quantify why the mismatch occurred. In these cases, it is crucial for the CDI specialist to have a coder who can help him or her understand what happened. During the course of this more in-depth investigation, the CDI specialist may learn what documentation would have been required to assign the diagnosis the CDI specialist saw clinically. There are some cases where the mismatch may boil down to other dynamics, such as:

- The coders have the entire chart at the time of coding for review, instead of reviewing the chart at a snapshot point during the hospitalization

- The coders understand the nuances of coding rules and regulations that a CDI specialist may not

An example of mismatches, both concurrent as well as retrospective, is taking multiple diagnoses that meet the definition for the principal diagnosis into consideration (read more about rules governing principal diagnosis assignment in Chapter 3). Sometimes this can be more of a subjective viewpoint, and there may not be only one correct answer.

In some cases, the CDI specialist and coder may approach the physician advisor for a clinical clarification. In other cases, after further review and discussion, HIM may elect to recode or resequence the case. In all cases, the HIM department must have final say on coding determinations. It is legally responsible for the codes billed and, therefore, its opinion must be final when there are differences.

One nice side effect of the mismatch process is that it can serve as another quality check for accurate coding—an invaluable outcome in the current Recovery Auditor and regulatory environment.

Identify Program Targets

Hospital administrators will be looking for alternative query data—data that essentially substantiate the return on investment of program costs. Administrators want to know that the program pays for itself, recoups "lost" revenue, improves quality scores for physicians and the facility, and improves the capture of severity and mortality data. To do this, most CDI programs track:

- Case-mix index

- CC/MCC capture rates

Case-mix index metrics

Almost every program uses the case mix index as one metric of CDI program performance. The case mix index is the sum of all your facility's MS-DRG relative weights, divided by the number (volume) of Medicare cases for the year. A low case mix index may denote MS-DRG assignments that do not adequately reflect the resources used to treat Medicare patients, but it is important to remember that the case mix index is also affected by:

- Types of services provided by the hospital

- Volumes of medical and surgical cases

- DRG assignments

- Quality of documentation

- Changes in federal guidelines such as the reassignment of diagnoses as CCs/MCCs (e.g., when acute renal failure was reassigned from an MCC to a CC)[13]

Of the previous factors, only one can be influenced by the CDI team: documentation. And, due to the variability that exists from month to month, the case mix index should be considered a measurement over time rather than a barometer of a particular month's performance. If you decide to review your case mix index for short periods of time (e.g., per quarter), make sure you compare the quarter of interest to the previous year, as seasonal variation in healthcare affects the results.

Because surgical MS-DRGs are higher weighted than medical MS-DRGs (because the cost of the surgery is typically higher and therefore represented in higher RW), an increase in the volume of surgical cases can increase the overall case mix index. Conversely, when the volume of surgical cases is flat, and the case mix index increases, such an increase represents an increasing complexity of medical patients seen by the facility.

Keep economic factors in mind as well. During the recent recession, many people postponed elective surgeries and delayed healthcare, which negatively affected hospitals' case mix index, especially if they were considered a more elite or expensive healthcare provider in the community, as consumers looked for lower-cost alternatives.

When analyzing case mix index data, be sure to factor out extenuating circumstances. Look to assess data:

- With and without tracheostomies

- Seasonal shifts in diagnoses

- Volume of symptom or low-weighted DRGs

- Changes in surgical volumes (shifts of certain procedures to the outpatient setting)

- Recovery Auditor–targeted DRGs

- Pairs or triplets of DRGs

To neutralize the case mix index so that CDI impact can be extrapolated, the facility has to exclude diagnoses and/or procedures not influenced by CDI activities, such as mechanical ventilation, surgical procedures (with the possible exception of excisional debridements), tracheostomies, and organ transplants. None of these procedures can be influenced by documentation improvement efforts because they would almost certainly be performed regardless of the quality of the documentation.

In addition, surgical volume variances that are statistically different from month to month need to be excluded to arrive at the correct comparisons. For example, if all the cardiothoracic surgeons are attending a conference, the volume of coronary artery bypass surgeries will be down for a particular month. Another example is the influence of payer patterns for a particular procedure, such as bariatric surgery. A sudden change in presurgical approval certification guidelines may cause a sudden drop in the number of bariatric surgery admissions. It is not impossible for facilities to arrive at an accurate neutralized case mix index, but most facilities leave this calculation to outside consulting companies experienced in CDI program performance measurements.

Fluctuations in patient admissions and surgical staff/services make it difficult to use the case mix index as an accurate measurement of CDI programs' influence on overall facility finances. Believe it or not, a high volume of one-day stays can negatively impact case mix index, as these short-stay cases are often reimbursed under the lowest relative weight due to an absence of CCs and MCCs. As such, CDI is one of many departments that can impact case mix index. That's why case mix index is typically considered an organizational metric rather than a departmental one.

CC/MCC rates or APR-DRG levels

A more accurate way to capture CDI performance is through the use of CC/MCC capture rates and/or all-payer-refined (APR)-DRG relative weights, but, again, this information should not be used as standalone information; rather, it should be used in conjunction with other data, such as physician performance.

It can be assumed that if the quality of the documentation in the record is improved, the CC or MCC capture rate will increase. It would obviously be unrealistic to expect any facility to have a 100% MCC capture rate. And a 0% MCC capture rate would be equally unbelievable. A facility performing well would fall somewhere in between. Many CDI consulting firms use a benchmark of 50% to 58% for a combined medical CC/MCC capture rate and 50% to 55% for a combined surgical CC/MCC capture rate.

When looking at CC/MCC capture rates, consider them as a pair because an increase in the MCC capture rate will result in a decrease in the CC capture rate. The facility's CC/MCC capture performance can be considered a more reliable indicator of CDI success than, say, the overall case mix index or query percentage, since it does show that as documentation improves, so does the CC/MCC capture rate. The CC/MCC capture rate also correlates well with program performance when compared to query volumes.

If a program is successful with physician education for a particular topic—for example, decubitus ulcers—it would be logical to assume that as physicians demonstrate more specific wound documentation, the number of decubitus queries will decrease as the CC/MCC capture rate increases and levels off. The CC/MCC capture rate does affect case mix index in that a higher volume of DRGs with CCs or MCCs will naturally result in higher relative weights and in turn will result in a higher overall case mix index, but again, the case mix index must be neutralized to exclude non-CDI factors, such as those listed previously.

Most all of the CMS hospital value-based purchasing program (VBP) measures are risk adjusted, which means more precise documentation has a positive impact. Since the advent of the hospital IQR program (see Chapter 1 for more information of both of these programs) many facilities use the APR-DRG grouping system by 3M to measure the severity of illness (SOI) and risk of mortality (ROM) for their patients in an effort to better determine where to focus quality improvement efforts.

This DRG system contains elements not currently included in the MS-DRG system, such as the ability to incorporate multiple CCs or MCCs into the overall severity of illness (SOI)/risk of mortality (ROM) scores. Under the current MS-DRG system, only one CC or MCC is needed to elevate the DRG assignment to a higher level. Under the APR-DRG system, the final APR-DRG assignment depends not only on the principal diagnosis but also on the type and quantity of specific comorbidities paired with the principal diagnosis.

When considering the impact of CDI programs, leadership should take into account improvements in SOI/ROM and the positive impact this can have on VBP reimbursement. Hospitals can "group batch" patient populations overall and by service line to determine a baseline measurement. These same reports can then be run on a quarterly or biannual basis for monitoring purposes and compared to VBP measures on a yearly basis to approximate the impact of CDI efforts.

Analyzing Data

A CDI program "task force" or committee including CDI specialists, coders, case managers, quality staff members, and leadership should meet regularly to discuss documentation improvement targets and review data. This group should discuss successes, operational issues, and problematic physicians.

Additionally, changes in clinical indicators, coding guidance, or difficult cases should be brought forward to provide education for those involved in the CDI process. This committee should analyze and identify troublesome patterns and formulate action plans. In collaboration with the CDI program manager/director, this committee can help communicate results to the hospital board of directors, the medical staff, or others.

Peer reviews

Every CDI program should objectively evaluate the outcomes, processes, and compliance of their CDI efforts. Auditing and monitoring provides oversight for the CDI program, insight into physician documentation and collaboration, and objective evaluation of the performance and effectiveness of individual CDI staff members as measured against your facility's policies and priorities.[14]

AHIMA's "Managing an Effective Query Process" states:

> Healthcare entities should consider establishing an auditing and monitoring program as a means to improve their query processes.[15]

Facilities that rely too heavily on consultants (or those who rely on consultants without overseeing their methods) may find their programs under government scrutiny. As the adage goes, "Ignorance of the law is no excuse." If inappropriate practices and inaccurate data are promulgated, it is the facility's responsibility to investigate the processes that led to the inaccuracies and to apply corrective actions.[16]

CDI managers will need to decide which queries to review and how to track the analysis. In many situations a simple Excel® spreadsheet can do the trick, although many facilities rely on electronic query systems or vendors to supply the raw data.

To create a statistically valid audit, you'll need to pull a reasonably wide selection of queries to review. For example, to figure out how frequently clinical indicators are used on queries, pull five charts from each staff member. Based on ACDIS benchmarking surveys, a monthly volume of 150 to 250 new cases and a query rate of 20% provide 30 to 50 queried cases. If a 10% random review rate is established as a goal, then five cases per CDI specialist per month should represent a reasonable audit plan. Choose five queries from five cases or days at random. This protects your review and the staff member from the risk that an outlier event (e.g., an unexpected illness or ill temper) will skew overall findings.

A sample audit form that identifies elements required for review is included in the appendix of this book.

Audits need not be a strictly managerial effort. Peer-to-peer reviews can provide an opportunity for CDI staff members to learn from each other, to see what each other is doing and support process improvement.[17]

In summary, a successful CDI program and physician query process involves bringing together the knowledge of many individuals with various training and expertise. It requires thorough and consistent review of ongoing trends within healthcare regulatory and reimbursement realms. An effective query practice requires not only the review of industry guidance but the incorporation of that guidance within the CDI department's policies and procedures.

Furthermore, the expertise of each individual within the healthcare processes—from coder, to physician advisor, to CDI specialist—each offers an invaluable insight as to how to craft compliant, clinically relevant query. Team involvement is crucial for the immediate and ongoing success of the program. Building a strong sense of teamwork through establishment of a vision, goals, and recognition will allow the hospital to leverage this knowledge and build a program that functions at the highest level with the greatest rate of return.

As indicated in the introduction of this book, queries must be compliant, but every query, when considerately and ethically crafted, deserves an answer.

REFERENCES

1. Centers for Medicare & Medicaid Services (CMS). Inpatient Prospective Payment System (IPPS) Final Rule. *www.cms.hhs.gov /AcuteInpatientPPS/downloads/CMS-1533-FC.pdf*, p. 208.

2. American Health Information Management Association (AHIMA). "Guidance for Clinical Documentation Improvement Programs," *Journal of AHIMA*, Vol. 81, No.5, May 2010. *http://library.ahima.org/xpedio/groups/public/documents/ahima/bok1_047343 .hcsp?dDocName=bok1_047343*.

3. Kruse, M. Taillon, H. *The Clinical Documentation Improvement Specialist's Handbook,* Second Edition. HCPro. Danvers, Mass., 2011.

4. Association of Clinical Documentation Improvement Specialists (ACDIS). "CDI efforts in the ED need not be traumatic." *CDI Journal*, Vol. 5 No. 3, July 2011. *www.hcpro.com/content/268140.pdf*.

5. ACDIS. "Q&A: Using case-mix index to track CDI efforts." *CDI Strategies*, Vol. 7, No. 5, February 28, 2013. *www.hcpro.com/acdis /archive.cfm?topic=WS_ACD_STG*.

6. AHIMA. "Managing an Effective Query Process." *Journal of AHIMA*, Vol. 79, No. 10, October 2008.

7. Ibid.

8. ACDIS. "RACs request queries as complex reviews roll out." *CDI Journal*, Vol. 4, No. 3, July 2010. *www.hcpro.com/content/253342.pdf*.

9. AHIMA. "Managing an Effective Query Process." *Journal of AHIMA*, Vol. 79, No. 10, October 2008.

10. ACDIS. "Q&A: Defining Physician Agreement." *ACDIS Blog*. March 13, 2013. *http://blogs.hcpro.com/acdis*.

11. AHIMA. "Guidelines for Achieving a Compliant Query Practice." *Journal of AHIMA*, Vol. 84, No. 2, February 2013. *http://library .ahima.org/xpedio/groups/public/documents/ahima/bok1_050018.hcsp?dDocName=bok1_050018*.

12. American Hospital Association. *Coding Clinic for ICD-9-CM, First Quarter, 2000*.

13. ACDIS. "Q&A: Using case-mix index to track CDI efforts." *CDI Strategies*, Vol. 7, No. 5, February 28, 2013.

14. ACDIS. "White Paper: Audit your CDI program to avoid pitfalls." *CDI Journal*, July 2011. *www.hcpro.com/content/268350.pdf*.

15. AHIMA. "Managing an Effective Query Process." *Journal of AHIMA*, Vol. 79, No. 10, October 2008.

16. ACDIS. "Conduct peer audits to provide query practice insight." *CDI Journal*, Vol. 7, No. 1, January 2013. *www.hcpro.com /content/288079.pdf*.

17. ACDIS. "White Paper: Audit your CDI program to avoid pitfalls." *CDI Journal*, July 2011. *www.hcpro.com/content/268350.pdf*.

Appendix

FIGURE A.1 ◇ OFFICIAL GUIDELINES FOR CODING AND REPORTING

Editor's note: The following Official Guidelines for Coding and Reporting *applicable under* ICD-9-CM *offer advice about how to query.*

B. 16	Resolve conflicting information concerning the body mass index, staging of ulcers, and their underlying conditions (e.g., obesity, malnutrition, pressure sores)
C. 1. b. 1) (a)	Differentiate between septicemia, the systemic inflammatory response syndrome (SIRS), sepsis (SIRS due to infection), and severe sepsis (sepsis with associated organ dysfunction)
C. 1. b. 2) (c)	Ascertain whether septicemia (sepsis) is present at the time of inpatient admission
C. 1. b. 4) (b)	Ascertain whether sepsis is present along with septicemia
C. 1. b. 5)	Ascertain a direct link between sepsis and any coexisting organ dysfunctions
C. 1. b. 7)	Ascertain whether a patient still has sepsis or septicemia even though the blood culture may be negative or inconclusive
C. 7. e. 2)	Ascertain the location of an acute myocardial infarction if only non-transmural or ST-segment elevation myocardial infarction is documented
C. 8. c. 3)	Clarify the principal diagnosis if the documentation is not clear as to whether acute respiratory failure and another condition are equally responsible for occasioning the admission
C. 10. a. 2)	Clarify whether post-transplant conditions are complications when the documentation is not clear
C. 12. a. 3)	Determine the stage of any pressure sore that is not documented in the record
C. 12. a. 8)	Determine whether the documentation is unclear as to whether the patient has a current (new) pressure ulcer or whether the patient is being treated for a healing pressure ulcer
C. 17. b. 4)	Determine the order of severity of multiple fractures
C. 17. f. 2) (b)	Clarify whether a patient's chronic kidney disease is related to a complication of a transplant
C. 17. f. 3) (a)	C. 17. f. 3) (a) – Clarify whether a patient's pneumonia is a complication of a ventilator
C. 17. g	If acute organ dysfunction is documented in the setting of non-infectious conditions, but it cannot be determined whether the acute organ dysfunction is associated with SIRS or is due to another condition (e.g., directly due to the trauma), the provider should be queried

FIGURE A.1 ◇ OFFICIAL GUIDELINES FOR CODING AND REPORTING (CONT.)

B	Determine whether laboratory findings are outside the normal range and the attending provider has ordered other tests to evaluate the condition or prescribed treatment to determine whether the abnormal findings should be added
Appendix I	Clarify issues related to the linking of signs/symptoms, timing of test results, and timing of findings
Appendix I	Clarify whether a condition is present on admission (POA)
Appendix I	General Medical/Surgical Examples – 14 – Determine the POA status of a pressure sore not documented at the time of admission

FIGURE A.2 ◇ **OFFICIAL GUIDELINES FOR CODING AND REPORTING FOR ICD-10-CM**

I.A.13	For conditions having an underlying etiology and multiple body system manifestations, ICD-10-CM convention requires sequencing the underlying condition first followed by the manifestation, unless there is a note by the manifestation code to sequence first.
1.B.7	"Code first" notes are also under certain codes that are not specifically manifestation codes but may be due to an underlying cause. When there is a "code first" note and an underlying condition is present, the underlying condition should be sequenced first. "Code, if applicable, any causal condition first", notes indicate that this code may be assigned as a principal diagnosis when the causal condition is unknown or not applicable. If a causal condition is known, then the code for that condition should be sequenced as the principal or first-listed diagnosis.
1.B.10	Coding of sequela generally requires two codes with the following sequencing: The condition or nature of the sequela is sequenced first. The sequela code is second. Exceptions are: cerebrovascular disease, complication of pregnancy, childbirth and the puerperium, and application of 7th characters for Chapter 19,
I.B.14	Documentation for BMI, Non-pressure ulcers and Pressure Ulcer Stages has not changed. May use information from other clinicians involved in the care of the patient. The associated diagnosis must still be documented by the provider. If there is conflicting information, query the provider.
1.B.16	Complications of care must have a cause-and-effect relationship between the care provided and the condition, and an indication in the documentation that it is a complication. If the complication is not clearly documented, query the provider
1.C.d.1.a.i	Negative or inconclusive blood cultures do not preclude a diagnosis of sepsis in patients with clinical evidence of the condition; however, the provider should be queried.
1.C.d.1.a.il	Urosepsis does not have a default code, and must be queried for clarification
1.C.d.1.a.iv	An acute organ dysfunction must be associated with the sepsis in order to assign the severe sepsis code. Query the provider if the documentation is not clear as to whether the acute organ dysfunction is related to the sepsis vs. another medical condition
1.C.2.c.1	The malignancy is sequenced first when anemia is associated with the malignancy, and the treatment is only for anemia. The anemia will be coded second.
1.C.2.c.1c.3	Dehydration is sequenced first when due to malignancy with only the dehydration being treated
1.C.4.a.5.a and b	Complications of insulin pumps are further classified by secondary codes to indicate under vs. overdose, intentional vs. non-intentional, with additional codes used to indicate the associated complication.
1.C.6.a	Includes rules for assigning dominate vs. non-dominate side for hemi and mono paresis and plegia. If not documented, the left side defaults to non-dominate unless the physician indicates the patient is ambidextrous
1.C.9.a.1	Hypertensive heart disease must have documentation of a causal relationship to assign the codes for hypertensive heart disease. The CHF codes will be coded and sequenced as secondary codes.

FIGURE A.2 ◇ OFFICIAL GUIDELINES FOR CODING AND REPORTING FOR ICD-10-CM

1.C.9.a.2	The relationship between CKD and HTN may be assumed if both conditions are present and the hypertensive chronic kidney disease codes should be used with a secondary code to indicate the stage of CKD.
1.C.9.a.3	The codes in category I13, Hypertensive heart and chronic kidney disease should be used to identify patients with hypertension, heart disease and chronic kidney disease. While the relationship between CKD and HTN can be assumed, the documentation must specify if there is a causal relationship between the HTN and heart failure
1.C.9.b	A Causal relationship can be assumed in a patient with both atherosclerosis and angina pectoris, unless the documentation indicates the angina is due to something else
1. C.9.e. 1 thru 4	Provides the rules for coding STEMI vs. NSTEMI myocardial infarction (MI) and defines subsequent MI as a patient who has suffered a new (second) AMI within 4 weeks of the initial (first) AMI
1.C.10.d.1	The documentation must specify "ventilator associated pneumonia" to use this code. Secondary codes should be used to identify the organism
1.C.12.a.5	The provider should be queried if the documentation is unclear whether the patient has a current (new) pressure ulcer or if the patient is being treated for a healing pressure ulcer
1.C.13.d.1-2	Osteoporosis codes should be assigned based on presence or absence of a pathological fracture. A current pathological fracture should be assigned even if the patient had a minor fall or trauma that would not usually break a normal healthy bone. The code for history of a healed osteoporosis fracture should be used in appropriate cases
1.C.14.a.2	If the documentation is unclear as to whether the patient has a complication of the transplant vs. CKD due to a not fully restored kidney function, query the provider.
1.C.18.a-b	Rules for coding of symptom diagnoses
1.C.18.a-g	Assign the SIRS due to non-infectious process codes when SIRS is documented with a non-infectious condition. Query the provider if acute organ dysfunction is present and the documentation is unclear as to SIRS vs. trauma as the cause
	Covers the rules for applying a 7th character to injury codes to clarify initial vs. subsequent encounter vs. sequela of an injury
1.C.19.e	Covers the rules for coding adverse effect vs. poisoning with the rules of code sequencing the same as they were in ICD-9-CM. New in ICD-10-SM is that the poisoning codes have an associated intent as their 5th or 6th character (accidental, intentional self-harm, assault and undetermined.
Appendix 1	Reporting requirement and clarifying if conditions were present on admission

FIGURE A.3 ◇ CODING CLINIC GUIDELINES

Editor's note: The following Coding Clinic *publications in reverse chronological order offer advice about how and when to query.*

July–August 1984, pages 12–17:	Determine whether "history of hypertension" means controlled on diet and/or medication.
July–August 1984, pages 17–19:	Determine whether the diagnosis of COPD and chronic bronchitis can be classified as obstructive chronic bronchitis or chronic obstructive emphysematous bronchitis, 491.2.
Fourth Quarter 1989, page 13:	Determine the etiology of ascites and pleural effusions in the setting of pancreatic neoplasms.
Fourth Quarter 1991, pages 14–16:	Differentiate between late Lyme disease and a late effect of (cured) Lyme disease.
First Quarter 1992, pages 15–16:	When deep venous thrombosis alone is documented, differentiate between it and deep venous thrombophlebitis if its clinical symptoms are present.
September 1992, page 13:	Determine the specific diagnosis being treated in repetitive motion syndrome.
Second Quarter 1992, pages 15–16:	If the physician documents anemia in the medical record some time after the operative episode, but does not state "postoperative" or "complication," query the physician as to whether the anemia can be further specified.
Fourth Quarter 1992, page 24:	Clarify the episode of care for acute myocardial infarction (acute, non-acute but less than eight weeks, or over eight weeks).
First Quarter 1993, page 24:	Coders should query the attending physician if, after reviewing the record, questions remain concerning prescribed medications that may indicate a specific condition.
First Quarter 1993, page 18:	The coder should not arbitrarily add an additional diagnosis to the final diagnostic statement on the basis of an abnormal laboratory finding alone. To make a diagnosis on the basis of a single lab value or abnormal diagnostic finding is risky and carries the possibility of error. Remember to always query the physician regarding the specific diagnosis being treated if it is not clearly stated in the medical record.
First Quarter 1993, page 17:	Determine whether common occurrences following cholecystectomy are postoperative complications.
Fourth Quarter 1993, page 43:	Determine whether any exacerbation of COPD in the postoperative period is a complication of surgery.

© 2013 HCPro, Inc.

FIGURE A.3 ◇ **CODING CLINIC GUIDELINES (CONT.)**

Fourth Quarter 1993, page 34:	Determine the chronicity of blood loss anemia if the documentation is unclear.
Fourth Quarter 1993, page 39:	Determine the underlying cause of pneumonia in the setting of abnormal sputum studies.
Fourth Quarter 1993, pages 39–40:	Determine any cause and effect between cardiac catheterization and myocardial infarctions occurring during this procedure.
Fourth Quarter 1993, pages 40–41:	Clarify the cause and effect of acute myocardial infarction in the setting of occluded coronary artery bypass grafts and native vessel disease.
Fifth Issue 1993, pages 6–7:	If the physician documents postoperative hypertension in the medical record, query the physician to determine whether the hypertension was related to or was a complication of the procedure.
Fifth Issue 1993, pages 17–24:	Clarify the nature of unspecified angina pectoris.
First Quarter 1994, page 7:	Determine the intent and site of shunt insertions.
First Quarter 1994, pages 13–14:	Determine the nature of physiologic jaundice in newborns when there is no other related diagnosis or treatment.
Second Quarter 1994, page 8:	Determine the status of any malignancy or disease upon removal of Hickman catheters after cancer chemotherapy.
Second Quarter 1994, page 17:	Determine the cause and effect of diabetes mellitus and peripheral vascular disease.
Third Quarter 1994, page 6:	Determine the effect that cocaine may have on an infant (e.g., toxic effects or withdrawal).
Fifth Issue 1994, page 11:	Determine the indication of any prescribed medication (e.g., oral potassium for hypokalemia).
Fifth Issue 1994, page 7:	Determine whether postoperative fever is a complication of surgery.
Second Quarter 1995, pages 14–15:	Determine the clinical significance of abnormal radiological findings (e.g., carotid stenosis) and their relationship to a documented condition (e.g., stroke).
Second Quarter 1995, page 17:	Determine whether coronary artery disease is of native or bypassed arteries if documentation is unclear concerning previous coronary artery bypass surgery.
Third Quarter 1995, page 6:	Determine whether chronic mental disorders "in remission" are truly resolved and warrant a V-code or another diagnosis code.

FIGURE A.3 ◇ CODING CLINIC GUIDELINES (CONT.)

Third Quarter 1995, page 13:	Clarify what symptoms constitute the toxicity of any particular drug (e.g., Dilantin) when they are not otherwise documented. (**Note:** ICD-9-CM 995.2 – Unspecified adverse effect of drug, medicinal, and biological substance – should never be coded on inpatients.)
Second Quarter 1996, pages 13–15:	Determine the circumstances of admission as to correctly sequence unclear relationships between gallstones and pancreatitis.
Second Quarter,1997, page 12:	Determine the exact consequences of adverse drug reactions.
Second Quarter 1997, page 14:	Determine whether patients with insulin-dependent diabetes mellitus have Type 1 or Type 2 diabetes.
First Quarter 1998, pages 11–12:	Determine whether specified treatment received during a hospitalization constitutes palliative care.
Second Quarter 1998, pages 3–7:	Determine the causal organisms of pneumonia in the setting of abnormal laboratory or radiology findings or the use of specified pharmaceuticals.
Fourth Quarter 1998, pages 88–89:	Determine the etiology of chronic neurological symptoms (e.g., left arm weakness) in the setting of old stroke (CVA).
Second Quarter 1999, page 9:	Determine the specific histology of tumors reported on pathology reports.
Third Quarter 1999, pages 4–5:	Determine whether gastroenteritis is infectious.
Third Quarter 1999, page 19–20:	Determine the nature of any underlying thyroid disease for patients labeled as "euthyroid."
First Quarter 2000, page 24:	Requirement to develop guidelines for when physician clarification should be requested, irrespective of the payer.
Second Quarter 2000, pages 17–18:	Requirement to query when the documentation is incomplete, vague, and contradictory.
Second Quarter 2000, page 15:	Requirement to query the attending physician when there is conflicting information from other treating physicians.
Second Quarter 2001, page 4:	Requirement to query if it is unclear whether clinical conditions after a Nissen fundoplication are complications.
Second Quarter 2002, page 13:	Requirement to determine whether "poorly controlled" diabetes is indicative of uncontrolled diabetes.
Second Quarter 2002, pages 17–18:	Requirement to query to determine the clinical significance of abnormal radiology, laboratory, or pathological findings. Subsequent *Coding Clinic* advice (2nd Quarter, 2004, page 14) emphasizes that coders cannot interpret clinical laboratories to determine their ICD-9-CM code.

FIGURE A.3 ◇ **CODING CLINIC GUIDELINES (CONT.)**

Second Quarter 2003, pages 7–8:	Requirement to determine the cause and effect of pleural effusions in the setting of systemic lupus erythematosis.
First Quarter 2004, page 18:	Determine whether patients with epilepsy are intractable.
First Quarter 2004, pages 18–19:	Expression that queries of attending physicians are not necessary if diagnoses are established by other treating physicians; however, queries are required if there is a conflict.
Second Quarter 2004, pages 4–5:	Determine whether any documented malignancy (e.g., renal carcinoma) is a primary lesion or a metastasis.
First Quarter 2005, page 5:	Clarify the principal diagnosis when unclear documentation confuses principal diagnosis assignment for patients admitted with acute respiratory failure and congestive heart failure.
Second Quarter 2005, pages 10–11:	Clarify whether left heart catheterization is performed when only internal pressure measurements and ventricular function are performed.
Third Quarter 2005, page 23:	Resolve ambiguity between septic shock and sepsis with hypotension.
Third Quarter 2005, page 17:	Determine whether rectal bleeding in the setting of hemorrhoids is due to the hemorrhoids or is incidental.
Third Quarter 2005, pages 16–17:	Determine whether "fever" alone in the postoperative period is a complication of surgery.
Third Quarter 2005, pages 17–18:	Determine the source of GI bleeding in the setting of abnormal endoscopic findings if not otherwise linked.
Third Quarter 2005, pages 18–19:	Determine the indication for a medication prescribed by telephone order.
Third Quarter 2005, pages 19–20:	Clarify any diagnosis that may not be valid.
First Quarter 2006, page 9:	Determine the exact nature of a patient's injury in the event an ordered physician states only that a patient has trauma.
First Quarter 2006, pages 7–8:	Clarify the nature of pathological findings reported on inpatient pathology reports.
Third Quarter 2006, pages 3–4:	Clarify the nature of acute conditions treated in the rehabilitation setting (acute stroke was excluded since this should be assigned as late effect of stroke codes in the rehabilitation setting).
First Quarter 2007, page 19:	Determine the exact nature of chest pain of gastrointestinal origin.

FIGURE A.3 ◇ **CODING CLINIC GUIDELINES (CONT.)**

Second Quarter 2007, pages 11–12:	Determine whether intraoperative seromuscular tears are complications of surgery (incidental durotomies during spine surgery were excluded from the need to query since these are automatically coded to 349.1).
Third Quarter 2007, pages 8–9:	Clarify whether symptoms are integral to an underlying condition if documentation is unclear.
First Quarter 2008, page 4:	Clarify whether debridement not otherwise specified is excisional or nonexcisional.
Third Quarter 2008, page 14:	Determine the reason for thiamine injections when the documentation is unclear.
Third Quarter 2008, pages 20–21:	Determine the time of onset of pressure sores if otherwise not clear.
Third Quarter 2008, pages 10–11:	Determine whether end-stent stenosis of coronary stents involves the stent itself or a vessel adjacent to the stent.
Third Quarter 2008, pages 14–15:	Emphasize that it is inappropriate to query for a medication taken prior to a hospitalization (e.g., Viagra) in the absence of other information in the medical record indicating the clinical significance of the underlying diagnosis (e.g., diabetic autonomic neuropathy).
Fourth Quarter 2008, pages 85–90:	Specify whether neuroendocrine (or any) tumor is benign or malignant.
First Quarter 2009, page 13:	Resolve conflict between the attending physician (e.g., an obstetrician) and a physician treating a newborn (e.g., a pediatrician) regarding term and preterm births.
First Quarter 2009, page 13:	Procure the recorded birth weight and estimated gestational age necessary for fifth-digit assignment for codes from category 764 and subcategories 765.0 and 765.1.
Third Quarter 2009, pages 16-17:	The term lobar pneumonia is outdated. Query the provider regarding the specific type of pneumonia and code accordingly based on the causal organism.
Fourth Quarter 2009, pages 85-87:	There is no specific timeframe that distinguishes acute from chronic pulmonary embolism. Query for clarification if the documentation is unclear.
Third Quarter 2010, pages 18-19.	Comfort care, and/or end of life care for terminally ill patient may be used to describe palliative care. If the documentation is unclear regarding palliative vs. non-palliative, query the provider.
Fourth Quarter 2010, page 135.	When hypertensive urgency is documented, query for the specific type of hypertension.

FIGURE A.3 ◇ CODING CLINIC GUIDELINES (CONT.)

First Quarter 2011, page 20:	If the physician documents "history of deep vein thrombosis and the patient is on Coumadin, query for prophylactic treatment vs. treatment for chronic DVT.
First Quarter 2011, pages 20-21:	If the patient has a Greenfield filter, clarify acute, chronic, or recurrent DVT if documentation is unclear.
First Quarter 2011, page 22:	Query the provider regarding if the documentation is unclear as to whether pancreatitis is infectious or noninfectious.
Second Quarter 2011, page 17:	Documentation of the clinical significance of adhesions may include numerous adhesions requiring a long time to lyse, extensive adhesions involving tedious lysis, extensive lysis, etc. If uncertainty exists regarding clinical significance, query the provider.
Fourth Quarter 2011, pages 184-185:	There must be a cause-and-effect relationship between the care provided and the condition, and an indication that it is a complication. Query the provider for clarification, if not clearly documented.
Third Quarter 2011, page 11:	Query the provider regarding brain compression when "mass effect" or "midline shift" is documented.
Second Quarter 2012, pages 20-21:	Query the provider regarding the cause of UTI when the patient has an indwelling catheter.
Second Quarter 2012, pages 21-22:	Query the physician to determine the specific condition(s) the patient has when "sepsis syndrome" is documented.
Third Quarter 2012, page 3:	Clarifies that the fact that a patient has two conditions that commonly occur together does not necessarily mean they are related. With the exception of hypertension and CKD, query the provider if it is not clear whether two conditions are related.
Third Quarter 2012, page 10:	If "moderate - severe malnutrition" is documented, query to determine if this means the malnutrition has progressed to severe vs. moderate not yet progressed to severe.
Third Quarter 2012, page 22:	Acute respiratory failure should be assigned based on the ED physician's diagnosis, however, if there is any conflicting or question of the diagnosis validity, query the provider.

FIGURE A.4 ◇ **SAMPLE CDI QUERY POLICY**

ABC MEDICAL CENTER		
ADMINISTRATIVE POLICY AND PROCEDURE MANUAL		No. XXX
CATEGORY: Documentation and Improvement Process DEPARTMENT: Compliance		No. XXXX
TITLE: Physician Inpatient Query Process		No. XXX.XX
Current Revision Date: xx/xx/xx Supersedes: N/A	Original Effective Date: xx/xx/xx	Page: X OF Y

SCOPE AND PURPOSE OF POLICY:

To clarify physician documentation whenever there is conflicting, ambiguous, or incomplete information in the medical record regarding any significant reportable condition or procedure.

1. <u>Reportable conditions</u> are defined by *Official Coding Guidelines* as those that affect patient care in terms of requiring:
   - Clinical evaluation; or
   - Therapeutic treatment; or
   - Diagnostic procedures; or
   - Extended length of hospital stay; or
   - Increased nursing care and/or monitoring.

2. Clinically significant conditions in the *newborn* include those listed above as well as those conditions that have implications for future health care needs.

3. As a result of the disparity in documentation practices by providers, querying has become a common communication and educational method to advocate proper documentation practices. Queries may be made in situations such as the following:
   a) Clinical indicators of a diagnosis but no documentation of the condition
   b) Clinical evidence for a higher degree of specificity or severity
   c) A cause-and-effect relationship between two conditions or organism
   d) An underlying cause when admitted with symptoms
   e) Only the treatment is documented (without a diagnosis documented)
   f) Present on admission (POA indicator status)

4. Only diagnosis codes that are clearly and consistently supported by provider documentation should be assigned and reported.

5. Only qualified individuals will be allowed to perform the query process who have strong competencies in the following areas:
   - Knowledge of healthcare regulations, including reimbursement and documentation requirements
   - Clinical knowledge with training in pathophysiology
   - Ability to read and analyze all information in a patient's health record
   - Established channels of communication with providers and other clinicians

FIGURE A.4 ◇ SAMPLE CDI QUERY POLICY (CONT.)

ABC MEDICAL CENTER	
ADMINISTRATIVE POLICY AND PROCEDURE MANUAL	No. XXX
CATEGORY: Documentation and Improvement Process DEPARTMENT: Compliance	No. XXXX
TITLE: Physician Inpatient Query Process	No. XXX.XX
Current Revision Date: xx/xx/xx Supersedes: N/A Original Effective Date: xx/xx/xx	Page: X OF Y

6. It is appropriate to generate a physician query when documentation in the patient's record fails to meet one of the following five criteria;
   - Legibility
   - Completeness
   - Clarity
   - Consistency
   - Precision

7. Queries may be either verbal or written and may be generated in one or more of the following ways:
   - Concurrent (while patient is still an inpatient)
   - Post-discharge
   - Post-bill

8. A query will include the following information
   - Patient name
   - Admission date and/or date of service
   - Health record number
   - Account number
   - Date query initiated
   - Name and contact information of the individual initiating the query
   - Statement of the issue in the form of a question along with clinical indicators specified from the patient's record

9. Queries must be written with precise language, identifying clinical indications from the health record and asking the provider to make a clinical interpretation of these facts based on his or her professional judgment of the case.

10. The query format should not sound presumptive, directing, prodding, probing, or as though the provider Is being led to make an assumption.

11. Queries will be designed to be in accord with recommendations as provided in "Managing an Effective Query Process" published by the American Health Information Management Association (AHIMA).

FIGURE A.4 ◇ SAMPLE CDI QUERY POLICY (CONT.)

ABC MEDICAL CENTER	
ADMINISTRATIVE POLICY AND PROCEDURE MANUAL	No. XXX
CATEGORY: Documentation and Improvement Process DEPARTMENT: Compliance	No. XXXX
TITLE: Physician Inpatient Query Process	No. XXX.XX

Current Revision Date: xx/xx/xx	Supersedes: N/A	Original Effective Date: xx/xx/xx	Page: X OF Y

12. Queries will be audited and monitored on a routine basis and the results of those audits will be kept in the department and provided to the Compliance Officer as needed.

13. This policy will be revised to remain in compliance with all State and Federal regulatory agencies.

Source: AHIMA. "Managing an Effective Query Process" *Journal of AHIMA 79*, No. 10 (October 2008): 83–88.

APPROVED:

Reviewed by:	Date

_____
XXXXX
Chief Financial Officer

_____
XXXXX
Director, Health Information Management

Source: ACDIS Form & Tools Library.

FIGURE A.5 ◇ COMPLIANCE PROCEDURES FOR CDI PRACTICE

ABC MEDICAL CENTER	
CLINICAL DOCUMENATION MANAGEMENT DEPARTMENT POLICY AND PROCEDURE MANUAL	No. XXX
CATEGORY: Documentation Improvement DEPARTMENT: Compliance Process	No. XXXX
TITLE: Clinical Documentation Compliance Practices	No. XXX.XX
Current Revision Date: xx/xx/xx Supersedes: N/A Original Effective Date: xx/xx/xx	Page: X OF Y

PURPOSE: To establish Clinical Documentation Improvement compliance practices.

POLICY:

1) There are department policies and procedures related to the Clinical Documentation Management Program. The policies and procedures are located in the departmental policies and procedure manual.

2) Each Clinical Documentation Specialist (CDS) position and management position has a current and accurate job description.
(Attachment A)

3) CDS have access to external coding and clinical documentation improvement resources to discuss unusual, difficult or questionable cases. CDS should first discuss their question with the coder who assigned the codes. If the question cannot be resolved, the issue will be pursued according to the process developed by the coders and the CDS.

Additionally, it may be necessary to contact the central office of the American Hospital Association (*Coding Clinic*). The central office will respond to written coding questions faxed or mailed to its office. The fax number at the central office is 312/422-4583. The address is: Central Office on ICD-9-CM, Coding Advice, American Hospital Association, One North Franklin, Chicago, IL 60606.

For CPT coding questions, it may necessary to contact the AMA CPT Advisory Line (a service fee will be charged by the AMA for this service).

4) CDS adhere to the following process should they wish to report a suspected fraudulent practice or event:

- CDS need to make sure they have correct information, then research and document the situation fully.

- The CDS should discuss the suspicion with his/her manager first.

FIGURE A.5 ◇ COMPLIANCE PROCEDURES FOR CDI PRACTICE (CONT.)

ABC MEDICAL CENTER	
CLINICAL DOCUMENATION MANAGEMENT DEPARTMENT POLICY AND PROCEDURE MANUAL	No. XXX
CATEGORY: Documentation Improvement DEPARTMENT: Compliance Process	No. XXXX
TITLE: Clinical Documentation Compliance Practices	No. XXX.XX
Current Revision Date: xx/xx/xx Supersedes: N/A Original Effective Date: xx/xx/xx	Page: X OF Y

- If the situation is not resolved at that point, the coder is encouraged to report the issue to the HIM Director.

- Clinical Documentation Specialists and others are free to report all suspected fraudulent practices or events to the Corporate Compliance Officer without fear of recrimination.

- If the CDS is not comfortable following this process, he/she is encouraged to report the issue directly to the Corporate Compliance Officer.

- Due to the sensitive nature of some activities, employees are discouraged from discussing such information among peer groups and are encouraged to use the procedures outlined above to report information that can be best addressed through the appropriate channels.

5) Clinical Documentation Improvement processes are monitored to assure compliance. These processes are located in the department policy and procedure manual.

6) The Clinical Documentation Improvement Specialists complete periodic audits of inpatient electronic worksheets and physician queries. Results of these audits are kept in the department and will be provided to the Compliance Department as requested. Results are used to focus education provided by the Clinical Documentation Improvement or HIM staff.

7) Results of audits are used to identify areas needing additional education for the clinical documentation improvement staff, physician staff and coding staff.

8) When a CDS fails to meet a minimum standard of quality, the progressive discipline policy will be followed.

9) Resource and agency CDS are included in all aforementioned processes.

FIGURE A.5 ◇ COMPLIANCE PROCEDURES FOR CDI PRACTICE (CONT.)

ABC MEDICAL CENTER

CLINICAL DOCUMENATION MANAGEMENT DEPARTMENT POLICY AND PROCEDURE MANUAL	No. XXX
CATEGORY: Documentation Improvement	No. XXXX
DEPARTMENT: Compliance Process	
TITLE: Clinical Documentation Compliance Practices	No. XXX.XX

Current Revision Date: xx/xx/xx   Supersedes: N/A   Original Effective Date: xx/xx/xx   Page: X OF Y

APPROVED:

Reviewed by: Date

_____
XXXXX
Chief Financial Officer

_____
XXXXX
Director, Health Information Management

Source: ACDIS Form & Tools Library.

FIGURE A.6 ◇ SAMPLE QUERIES

DRAFT HEART FAILURE PROGRESS NOTE

1) What is the LVEF (left ventricular ejection fraction) if not done during this admission? _____

_____

2) Acuity:
- ❏ Acute
- ❏ Acute on chronic
- ❏ Chronic
- ❏ Unknown

3) Type:

Left ventricular failure (type):
- ❏ Systolic
- ❏ Diastolic
- ❏ Systolic and diastolic
- ❏ Right ventricular systolic failure
- ❏ Unknown

4) Is cardiomyopathy present?
- ❏ Yes
- ❏ No

5) What is the cause(s)?
- ❏ Alcohol/substance abuse
- ❏ Diabetes
- ❏ Hypertension
- ❏ Ischemia
- ❏ Valvular
- ❏ IHSS or primary
- ❏ Toxic
- ❏ Unknown
- ❏ Other, please document: _____

6) Is an ACE inhibitor/ARB prescribed if LVEF is less than 40%?
- ❏ Yes
- ❏ No

FIGURE A.6 ◇ SAMPLE QUERIES (CONT.)

7) If no, contraindication to ACE inhibitor/ARB, please check all indications that are appropriate:

❏ Aortic stenosis—moderate or severe

❏ Renal insufficiency

❏ Potassium greater than 5.5—no ACE inhibitor/ARB

❏ ACE inhibitor/ARB allergy

❏ Severe hypotension with ACE inhibitor/ARB in past

❏ History ACE inhibitor/ARB—induced cough

❏ ACE inhibitor/ARB contraindicated

❏ Intolerant of ACE inhibitor/ARB

❏ Problems with ACE inhibitor/ARB in the past

❏ May start ACE therapy after blood pressure stabilizes

❏ Complaining of severe cough—will discontinue ACE inhibitor/ARB

❏ Patient refusing all medications

❏ Terminal care, no further treatment

❏ Other reason(s) _____

Comments:

_____

_____

_____

_____

_____   _____

Physician signature   Date

Source: James S. Kennedy

FIGURE A.6 ◇ SAMPLE QUERIES (CONT.)

DRAFT CHEST PAIN QUERY FOR CLINICAL INDICATIONS

Progress Note: Chest Pain Documentation Note

Dear Dr. _____.

You have documented **chest pain.** To accurately code this diagnosis and obtain important **core measure** information, we ask that you specifiy the **nature** and **cause(s)** of chest pain.

Please describe the nature of the patient's chest pain:

❏ Pleuritic	❏ Radicular	❏ Angina
❏ Postoperative	❏ Gallbladder	❏ Stable ❏ @Rest ❏ Unstable
❏ Heartburn	❏ Psychogenic	❏ Cannot be determined
❏ Musculoskeletal	❏ Pericardial	❏ Other:

Please describe the most likely underlying cause of the patient's chest pain
(**Note:** This will require dictation in the discharge summary since uncertain diagnosis cannot be coded unless documented at the time of discharge):

❏ CAD	❏ Pleurisy	❏ GERD
❏ Stent Complication	❏ Costochondritis	❏ PUD
❏ Accelerated HTN	❏ Rib Fracture	❏ Gallstones
❏ Pericarditis	❏ Neuritis	❏ Neuropathy 2°
❏ Drug Toxicity	❏ Cannot be determined	❏ Other

FIGURE A.6 ◇ SAMPLE QUERIES (CONT.)

DRAFT PNEUMONIA QUERY FOR CLINICAL INDICATIONS

PNEUMONIA ORDERS	
Date: Time:	Another brand of drug identical in form and content may be dispensed unless checked ❏
Diagnosis: Pneumonia (positive x-ray and/or convincing clinical circumstances)	
Suspected Bacterial etiology:	❏ Staph aureus–req. antistaph rx. ❏ Aspiration–req. anaerobic/gram-coverage ❏ Gram-negative rod–req. gram negative coverage ❏ Poss. Legionnaires ❏ Poss. H. Flu ❏ Other _____
Current risk factors:	❏ COPD ❏ +HIV ❏ Known AIDS ❏ Sickle-cell ❏ Alcoholism ❏ Drug Abuse ❏ Influenza ❏ Parkinson's Dz ❏ Malnutrition ❏ Immunocompromised State ❏ Malignancy - _____ ❏ Uncontrolled Diabetes ❏ Encephalopathy ❏ Dementia ❏ Unable to take po meds
Complex conditions present on admission:	❏ Sepsis (SIRS) (Temp > 101; WBC > 12K, left shift, and/or organ dysfunction) 2° infection ❏ Acute resp. failure ❏ Acute resp. distress ❏ Status asthmaticus ❏ Hypoxemia ❏ Significant pleural effusion ❏ Hypovolemia ❏ Encephalopathy ❏ Pressure Sore ❏ Chronic Kidney Disease–Stage ❏ ESRD ❏ Acute Renal Failure
Admission Status: ❏ Inpatient ❏ Observation **Admission to Attending Physician:**	**Admit Location:** ❏ Medical ❏ Telemetry ❏ ICU ❏ Notified

Source: James S. Kennedy

FIGURE A.7 ◇ SAMPLE QUERY AUDIT FORM

DEMOGRAPHIC Information

CDS	Admit date	D/C date	Encounter #	Reviewer
Date of review	Final working DRG	Billed DRG		

General CDI process items				
1	Initial review conducted <48 hrs	Yes	No	
2	Adequate re-reviews (dependent on clinical condition and documentation status; anywhere from daily to 2x weekly)	Yes	No	
3	Final working DRG (after any query resolution) matches billed DRG	Yes	No	
3 A	Appropriate PDX and procedures recognized	Yes	No	N/A
3 B	ODX influencing DRG assignment recognized	Yes	No	N/A
3 C	Significant ODX influencing ROM / SOI / LOS recognized	Yes	No	N/A
4	Relevant clinical factors were identified during reviews (pertinent positive & negative/normal) and relevant trends in documentation were recognized	Yes	No	
5	No missed query opportunity (details in comments) (alternative diagnosis were recognized, considered and either queried or appropriately refrained from query)	Yes	No	
6	Comments:			N/A

Query specific items (N/A if no query posed) Each query contains or complies with:				
7	If query forms utilized: appropriate form used AND form content was customized to the specific case documentation, circumstances and data	Yes	No	N/A
8	Nature of query (PDX, proc, CC/MCC, 2nd CC/MCC, SOI/ROM/LOS, Clarify, POA, etc.) is identified and recorded appropriately	Yes	No	N/A
9	Reason(s) for query: * The clinical symptoms, indicators or information are included; * The specific documentation issue is described (legibility, consistency, etc.) * Treatment is described that lacks a diagnosis * Other	Yes	No	N/A
10	The clinical indicators firmly support the query (i.e., not stretched) (including recognition and use of broadly recognized clinical literature standards)	Yes	No	N/A
11	Succinct, clear wording of the query with a clear question posed	Yes	No	N/A

FIGURE A.7 ◇ **SAMPLE QUERY AUDIT FORM (CONT.)**

12	Formatted in a user friendly manner (appropriate use of bullets, avoidance of run-on sentences, etc.)	Yes		
13	Timely presentation (i.e., adequate time for work up results to be in the record; initial physician documents must be in record prior to the query posed)	Yes	No	
14	Working DRG at time of query is appropriate to existent documentation	Yes	No	N/A
15	Suggested answer options are presented appropriately (Note: If was to confirm or rule out a diagnosis documented as possible/etc,. then format of options maybe appropriate to differ from standard multiple choice)	Yes	No	N/A
15A	Open ended question posed	Yes	No	N/A
15B	Multiple choice: **At least** 2 clinical reasonable for this pt diagnosis presented as options	Yes	No	N/A
15C	Multiple choice answer format: includes other _____ and clinically undertermined	Yes	No	N/A
16	Provider's response was appropriately recorded in tracking software or tool	Yes	No	N/A
17	**Final** result / impact of query appropriately recorded	Yes	No	N/A
18	Inclusion of required data elements (patient identifiers, person posing query, contact phone #, etc.)	Yes	No	N/A
19	Overall, query was **non-leading**	Yes	No	N/A
20	Other query comments:			

ADMINISTRATIVE SECTION

	Inter-rater reliability: 90% agreement on findings between 2 peers conducting reviews			
	If no, third level review 90% agreement with findings?			

Source: Butler, D. "Conduct peer audits to provide query practice insight." *CDI Journal,* January 2013.